AA

ORDNANCE SURVEY
LEISURE GUIDE
SOUTH DOWNS

Produced jointly by the Publishing Division of the
Automobile Association and the Ordnance Survey

Cover: Downs meet sea at the Seven Sisters, Exceat
Title page: Pyecombe's churchyard gate with crook
Contents page: Nymans, a National Trust garden
Introductory page: looking north towards South Harting

Editor: Rebecca Snelling

Copy editor: Russell P O Beach

Art editor: Dave Austin

Design assistants: Plum Design

Editorial contributors: Ruth Aldridge (Gazetteer);
J R Armstrong MBE, MA (Traditional Local Buildings);
Dr P L Drewett (Ancient Remains); J D Godfrey (Walks);
A J Hopkins (Shaping the Landscape, Woodland and
Downland Wildlife); Peter Wenham (Gardens of the
Downs and Weald); Angela Wigglesworth (Gazetteer);
Tony Youngs (Along the South Downs Way)

Directory compiled by the West Sussex County Council

Picture researcher: Wyn Voysey

Original photography: Martin Trelawny

Typeset by Avonset, Midsomer Norton, Bath.
Printed in Great Britain by Chorley & Pickersgill Ltd,
Leeds

Maps extracted from the Ordnance Survey's 1:625 000
Routeplanner map enlarged to a scale of 1:500 000,
1:250 000 Routemaster Series, also enlarged to
1:200 000, and 1:25 000 Pathfinder and Outdoor
Leisure Map Series, with the permission of Her
Majesty's Stationery Office. Crown Copyright reserved.

Additions to the maps by the Cartographic Dept of the
Automobile Association and the Ordnance Survey.

Produced by the Publishing Division of the Automobile
Association.

Distributed in the United Kingdom by the Ordnance
Survey, Southampton, and the Publishing Division of
the Automobile Association, Fanum House,
Basingstoke, Hampshire RG21 2EA.

AA ISBN 0 86145 667 X (hardback)
AA ISBN 0 86145 657 2 (softback)
OS ISBN 0 31900134 2 (hardback)
OS ISBN 0 31900133 4 (softback)

Published by the Automobile Association and the
Ordnance Survey.

AA Reference: 50788 (hardback)
AA Reference: 50775 (softback)

SOUTH DOWNS

Contents

Using this Book 4
Introduction 5
Shaping the Landscape 6
Ancient Remains 11
Along the South Downs Way 16
Woodland and Downland Wildlife 20
Traditional Local Buildings 23
Gardens of the Downs and Weald 27
A to Z Gazetteer 31
Directory 73
Atlas Legend 80 / Atlas 82
Motor Tours 88
Walks 94
Index 110

Using this Book

The entries in the Gazetteer have been carefully selected although for reasons of space it has not been possible to include every community in the region. A number of small villages are described under the entry for a larger neighbour, and these can be found by using the index.

Each entry in the A to Z Gazetteer has the atlas page number on which the place can be found and its National Grid reference included under the heading. An explanation of how to use the National Grid is given on page 80.

Beneath many of the entries in the Gazetteer are listed AA-recommended hotels, restaurants, garages, guesthouses, campsites and self-catering accommodation in the immediate vicinity of the place described.

For reasons of space the AA-recommended establishments under some entries are a selection only. For full details see the AA range of annual guides and the AA *Members' Handbook*.

HOTELS

1-star	Good hotels and inns, generally of small scale and with acceptable facilities and furnishing.
2-star	Hotels offering a higher standard of accommodation, with some private bathrooms/showers; lavatories on all floors; wider choice of food.
3-star	Well-appointed hotels; a good proportion of bedrooms with private bathrooms/showers.
4-star	Exceptionally well-appointed hotels offering a high standard of comfort and service, the majority of bedrooms should have private bathrooms/showers.
5-star	Luxury hotels offering the highest international standards.

Hotels often satisfy some of the requirements for higher classifications than that awarded.

Red-star	Red stars denote hotels which are considered to be of outstanding merit within their classification.
Country House Hotel	A hotel where a relaxed informal atmosphere prevails. Some of the facilities may differ from those at urban hotels of the same classification.

RESTAURANTS

1-fork	Modest but good restaurant.
2-fork	Restaurant offering a higher standard of comfort than above.
3-fork	Well-appointed restaurant.
4-fork	Exceptionally well-appointed restaurant.
5-fork	Luxury restaurant.
1-rosette	Hotel or restaurant where the cuisine is considered to be of a higher standard than is expected in an establishment within its classification.
2-rosette	Hotel or restaurant offering very much above average food irrespective of the classification.
3-rosette	Hotel or restaurant offering outstanding food, irrespective of classification.

GUESTHOUSES

These are different from, but not necessarily inferior to, AA-appointed hotels, and they offer an alternative for those who prefer inexpensive and not too elaborate accommodation. They all provide clean, comfortable accommodation in homely surroundings. Each establishment must usually offer at least six bedrooms and there should be a general bathroom and a general toilet for every six bedrooms without private facilities.

SELF CATERING

These establishments, which are all inspected on a regular basis, have to meet minimum standards in accommodation, furniture, fixtures and fittings, services and linen.

CAMPSITES

1-pennant	Site licence; 10% of pitches for touring units; site density not more than 30 per acre; 2 separate toilets for each sex per 30 pitches; good quality tapwater; efficient waste disposal; regular cleaning of ablutions block; fire precautions; well-drained ground.
2-pennant	All one-pennant facilities plus: 2 washbasins with hot and cold water for each sex per 30 pitches in separate washrooms; warden available at certain times of the day.
3-pennant	All two-pennant facilities plus: one shower or bath for each sex per 30 pitches, with hot and cold water; electric shaver points and mirrors; all-night lighting of toilet blocks; deep sinks for washing clothes; facilities for buying milk, bread and gas; warden in attendance by day, on call by night.
4-pennant	All three-pennant facilities plus: a higher degree of organisation than one–three-pennant sites; attention to landscaping; reception office; late-arrivals enclosure; first aid hut; shop; routes to essential facilities lit after dark; play area; bad weather shelter; hard standing for touring vans.
5-pennant	A comprehensive range of services and equipment; careful landscaping; automatic laundry; public telephone; indoor play facilities for children; extra facilities for recreation; warden in attendance 24 hours per day.

SOUTH DOWNS Introduction

Glorious chalk downland, rivers meandering down to the sea, wooded combes, timeless villages, historic towns and busy seaside resorts are all to be found within this beautiful area.

Lavishly illustrated, this guide describes both the past and the present and is packed with information on where to go and what to see – from wild flowers to windmills, from Chanctonbury Ring to Brighton Pavilion.

Written by people who know and love the area and backed by the AA's research expertise and the Ordnance Survey's superb mapping, this book is designed to be as appealing and useful to the first-time visitor as to those who are already familiar with the considerable charm of the South Downs.

Shaping the Landscape

A driver heading south-west out of London around the M25, then south along the A22, A24 or A3, is soon in a rolling landscape of small fields and farms, woods and winding hedgerows. These same roads once carried charabancs full of bank clerks, stevedores and their families whose only taste of the countryside might have been a yearly ride into Sussex, through copses and meadows, to the Downs and coast.

City-born descendants of these workers grew up with a special vision of the Downs, and today many make the same journey with a sense of nostalgia – in a fraction of the time it once took and with enough leisure to enjoy the rural heritage. It takes less than an hour to cross the Weald, still the most attractive wooded countryside in Britain. Then, quite suddenly, the trees melt away and a great curtain of downland is drawn across the skyline from east to west from Beachy Head in Sussex to Butser Hill in the next county.

Hampshire's Butser Hill, highest of the South Downs

Beneath a shallow sea

One hundred million years ago this part of Europe was covered by water, a shallow sea inhabited by anemones, ammonites and bivalves. For another 40 million years a layer of mud and shell fragments accumulated, until a series of earthquakes – which created the Alps and the Himalayas – thrust up what was by now a 1,000ft thick layer of chalk into an elongated dome, or anticline. Gradually the crest of the dome was eroded away, leaving a steep scarp slope facing inwards and a dip slope receding outwards. A map of north-west Europe shows the extent of the anticline, framed by downland. The English Channel is a recent phenomenon in geological terms, and the Weald stretched across to what is now northern France.

On the English side the White Cliffs of Dover mark the start of the North Downs, which arc across Kent and Surrey. Eventually the chalk hills swing south as the Hampshire Downs before turning east again as the South Downs and meeting the sea at the Seven Sisters. The scarp slope of the North Downs faces south, whilst the steeper slopes of the South Downs face north. The whole appearance of the Downs, including traditional patterns of farming and human settlement, reflect the nature of the land. Many old houses and barns are faced with flints, dug from chalk pits, and in wet weather the lanes and byways are edged by pale grey mud – yet there are few water-filled ditches or streams. Trees are tall, bushes are often covered with wild clematis and there is a strong sense of being somewhere different.

Right: a 20-minute planned walk on top of Beachy Head affords marvellous coastal views

Below: vernacular South Downs' architecture is preserved at the Weald and Downland Museum

Background: this painting by Fielding (1787–1855) illustrates the bare and treeless landscapes that resulted from intensive sheep husbandry

The highest point in the South Downs is Butser Hill, but altitude is relative. There are many lower places offering exhilarating views that turn out to be far more impressive than anticipated when read from a map. Fine panoramas exist from most of the high downland hill crests, but especially from Harting Down, Ditchling Beacon and Firle Beacon. Ancient man used such places for centuries as signal stations, to see and be seen. More recently, several points on the scarp were used as sites for windmills – the Clayton windmills, Jack and Jill, are especially good examples. Today, kites and hang-gliders harness the wind, and visitors from all over the country are attracted to the special beauty of the windswept ridge.

Seen from Midhurst or Hurstpierpoint, the South Downs seem immutable. In fact, chalk is soft and easily worn away. Only 10,000 years ago the most recent natural shaping of the land occurred as an aftermath of the Ice Age. For a million years most of Britain was little more than a frozen waste. However, the ice sheets eventually receded and improving temperatures resulted in torrents of meltwater which cut their way through frozen chalk. Eventually the chalk also thawed and the meltwater soaked underground; streams and rivers disappeared, leaving a network of dry valleys and coombs. Trees – juniper, hazel, oak and beech – tracked their way north and west from the Continent.

Wilderness transformed

About 7,500 years ago Britain became an island. Then, 6,000 years ago, the first farmers arrived. Modern naturalists, historians and geographers would give their eye teeth to be taken back in a time capsule and stand on the Downs in those far-off days, to see how the wilderness was gradually transformed into green fields. The Downs were among the first places to be settled by Neolithic

Views across the Weald, from 813ft Ditchling Beacon

farmers; it was much easier to clear beech trees from the thin dry soils of this area than oaks from the heavy Wealden clays to the north. Much more extensive clearance was carried out by Bronze and Iron Age farmers, and by Roman times wheat was being exported to France. However, grazing animals – especially sheep – became more and more important.

Sheep-farming reached its peak in the 15th and 16th centuries, and although it began to decline with the introduction of the four-course rotation, it was still dominant well into the present century. Domestic animals have varied feeding habits, affecting the landscape in different ways. Downland grazed by sheep is nibbled closely and evenly, whereas cattle are more selective and the resulting sward is more tufted. When grazing is constant

'Jill', a post-mill sited next to a tower-mill on the Downs at Clayton

The Great Fair at Lewes, shown in this 19th-century engraving, was a high spot in the sheep farmer's year

there are few trees or shrubs, because they are browsed off as saplings.

There is little doubt that most of the South Downs were once bare and featureless – a far cry from the wildwood of early Neolithic times. Even when sheep-rearing diminished, rabbits continued the process, cropping any vegetation to a stubble and keeping the slopes smooth. Then in the 1950s came myxomatosis; rabbit populations were slashed and for the first time in 1,000 years seedlings of bramble and hawthorn thrived. They grew into extensive tangles and thickets, reducing the open grazing dramatically and changing the visual impact of the countryside.

Inevitable change

It was inevitable that the Downs would change. Open grassland was an artificial phenomenon, a controlled phase in a succession that would run wild again given half a chance. It was an extended and fortunate interlude between what nature would or could do and what economic agriculture soon had in mind – namely a quantum leap forward to 'agribusiness' and intensive arable farming.

The romantic idyll of shepherds and swains tending their flocks like subjects in a Gainsborough painting was simple nonsense, as unrealistic as Victorian stories of happy contented miners or mill-workers. When sheep-rearing was pervasive, rural communities had a hard and rugged time of it. Nor was the landscape especially beautiful, since the heavy stocking of sheep on the hills was such that even in the 1920s the fields above Rottingdean were known as 'The Mutton Factory' – noisy and busy. But sheep created the Downs as they are known today, and the footpaths which cross them are usually along sheep-tracks of close-cropped turf.

The River Arun slices the Downs into two. West the area is quite heavily wooded, whilst to the east there are open rolling fields. Some still contain flocks of sheep, moved from field to field rather than left to roam the hill slopes, but most of the old pasture is now arable land. The need for self-

sufficiency in the Napoleonic Wars speeded up the trend from pastoral to arable farming, thence the ploughing of downland. World War II sealed this transformation. The size of the holdings – from 500 to 1,000 acres compared with 80 to 200 acres in the case of traditional dairy farms on the Wealden clays – and the sophistication of machinery and availability of chemical fertilisers have all contributed to the profitability of arable farming.

Today, barley is the principal crop, sown in October and harvested in August. The hazy green of the young corn in early spring and the swaying sea of yellow ears at harvest time can be impressive, an evocation of the countryside to a whole new generation of town-dwellers. Wheat is also grown, and some maize, but of all the arable crops it is oilseed rape which is the most noticeable. Fields full of its acid-yellow flowers create brilliant, eye-catching points of light visible for miles around. As with many other crops, however, oilseed rape is in surplus so unlikely to spread farther.

Field beans are sometimes grown for cattle, but in general cattle husbandry has declined. A few Friesian herds remain, and some store cattle are kept, but the markets at such towns as Lewes and Haywards Heath receive fewer and fewer animals. Perhaps the designation by the Minister of

Acres of oilseed rape seen from the top of Firle Beacon

Agriculture of the eastern area of the South Downs as an Environmentally Sensitive Area will encourage farmers to return to sheep husbandry at the expense of cattle or arable farming – though it is likely that many farmers will stay with the tried and trusted crops that have brought them prosperity over the past few decades.

Commercial pressures

The closeness of the South Downs to the vastness of London has made the area quick to react to changes or trends in the demands of sophisticated consumers. The observer standing on a high downland point and looking towards Chichester can see, not just the reflection of sunlight from the harbour, but also the reflections from acres of glasshouses covering expanses of Grade One agricultural land on the coastal plain. The guarantee of a ready market for horticultural specialities has transformed an area that might otherwise have been put down to wheat, maize or potatoes. Daffodils and roses are a much more lucrative proposition. By the same token, the changing tastes of the public have led to the virtual disappearance of the traditional breed of sheep, the Southdown. This stocky, woolly-faced beast is now only found on a couple of farms, one of which is near Ringmer – close to Glynde, where the breed was first established by John Ellman 100 years ago.

The only place to see Southdown sheep in large numbers today is in Central France; in Britain it went out of fashion for the simple reason that its progeny produce much too fatty a carcass, unacceptable to most people. Most farmers these days rear mule lambs, the result of a cross between Swaledale ewes and a Bluefaced Leicester ram. Another example of the sensitivity of food producers to the requirements of consumers has been the move away from intensive pig husbandry. The public outcry against factory farming has encouraged many farmers to keep their pigs in outdoor units. The foraging and trampling of a large number of these animals quickly reduces ground cover to a morass, and some hillsides west of the River Arun have come to resemble the old battlegrounds of the Western Front. Agriculture may change, but pigs will always be pigs.

Other resources

As with most other rural areas, agriculture is the most important element of land use in the South Downs, but it is by no means the only one. The exploitation of natural resources over past centuries has had its effect on the modern scene. Old quarries scar the hillsides – fascinating places now, providing a unique insight into the structure of the landscape, the thin 'Icknield' soils and white heart of the downland. Woodland has also been an important resource in times past, especially on the heavy 'gumboot' soils north of the chalk scarp. It took 1,000 oak trees to build a ship of the line like HMS *Victory*, and navy timber was of great strategic importance. Some oakwoods in the area were managed as high forest, others as coppice with standards, producing not only timber but also crops of rods and poles that were harvested every 12 or 14 years. This wood ('wood' rather than 'timber' – the two terms once had different meanings) was used to make hurdles, roofing spars and locally as the raw material for charcoal-burning. Fragments of coppiced woodland still exist, and at places such as West Dean Wood and Woods Mill the craft is demonstrated as a low-tech, ecologically acceptable alternative to intensive woodland management.

Block-planting of conifers is much more limited in Sussex than in most other counties, because the soils of the Downs are too dry and chalky. The only extensive plantations are absorbed into the general mix of woodland on the Wealden clays and sands. Many of the isolated stands of mature trees on the Downs themselves are of beeches, planted for commemorative purposes as memorials or celebrations. Sited with considerable care and forethought, they now make a vital impact on the skyline. The 'hangers' on the steeper slopes are especially imposing.

Enduring beauty

As easy travel and improved communication have opened Sussex to the ebb and flow of London life, so the county has become a complex blend of deep-rooted tradition and quick-silver reaction. The South Downs, framed between the Weald to the north and the Channel to the south, may now only be a picnic-ride away from the capital, but succeeding generations of visitors have found it the essence of rural England. It has changed, as any landscape is changed, by the impact of man – but its beauty is as fresh as ever.

Because people have come to prefer their lamb lean, the fatty Southdown breed has all but disappeared

R.Sands.fc.   Landfeer del

Ancient Remains

The hills and valleys of the Sussex Downs teem with ancient remains. Every break in their sinuous outline, however small, is the work of man, whether ancient or modern, and has a tale to tell if only we have eyes to read it aright. (Cecil Curwen, 1929).

The South Downs as seen today, a rolling expanse of low hills and dry valleys, constitute a man-made landscape. No inch of it has not been changed by man. When in about 300,000 BC the earliest 'Britons' knapped flints and hunted on the grassy plain at Boxgrove, the Downs were densely wooded. The last Ice Age destroyed that woodland, and through a period of intense cold remodelled the hills into roughly the form in which they appear today. But between then and now the tree cover rapidly recovered, so that by 10,000 BC the Downs were once again woodland.

Into this new woodland came Middle Stone Age hunters, following the fleet-footed red deer, elk, roe deer and wild pig, leaving behind the finely-worked microlithic hunting tools that can be seen in all Sussex museums. These hunters cleared patches in the woodland, camped for a night and moved on. They lived in harmony with nature, allowing the wooded downland to survive – for this was their larder.

Earliest farmers

Farmers arrived on the Downs a little before 4,000BC, rapidly spreading eastwards with devastating effect on the fragile downland landscape. Large tracts of wood were cleared for crop planting and grazing animals, the population exploded and great defended villages were constructed on The Trundle and at Whitehawk to protect fields and herds. These earthwork enclosures – with ditches 2yds deep, high banks, and great wooden gates – dominated the landscape. Around them were endlessly-shifting patterns of small farms where – as on Bishopstone Hill – family groups grew emmer wheat and six-row barley, kept cattle, pigs and sheep and perhaps continued to hunt wild deer. They added to their crops fat hen, burdock, chickweed and shellfish. Felling the woodland on the Downs and elsewhere required many strong flint axes, so the West Sussex Downs became a mining centre for flint. Dozens of vertical shafts were sunk through the chalk to seams of the mineral, and from the shafts were dug side galleries. Complexes of pits at Cissbury, Harrow Hill and Windover Hill still clearly show the activities of these first miners.

A controlling force in this Neolithic society was certainly religion, and probably a veneration of ancestors who first settled the land. Long barrows and small enclosures survive as part of a complex of religion, ceremony and burial practices. Long barrows, some like Bevis's Thumb in West Sussex, are great mounds up to 70yds long, with deep flanking ditches cut over 2yds into the solid chalk. They fulfilled a burial and religious role, perhaps where ancestors' remains were stored and venerated. At least 16 still exist, and the finest can be visited at Bevis's Thumb, Compton, and Windover Hill – overlooking the Saxon village of Alfriston.

View from Windover Hill, a source of flint in early times

Prehistoric tools shown in the Barbican Museum at Lewes, including flint axes and scrapers

Small ritual enclosures were also constructed as part of Neolithic death rites. These – of which examples survive on Combe Hill, Offham, Bury Hill, and at Barkhale – were built in areas not yet cleared of woodland. Bits of broken human bone found in them suggest that they may have been designed for the exposure of dead bodies on the surface of the ground. Bones picked clean by animals were then perhaps collected for use in rituals at the long barrows where they are found.

Bronze and barrows
About 2,500 BC began the construction of a new type of burial and religious monument, the round barrow, of which over 1,000 were built in Sussex, but today only a few hundred remain. The most spectacular group surviving is that of the Devil's Jumps on Treyford Hill, where five huge round mounds with encircling ditches dominate the landscape. Most of these barrows have produced just a few hundred bones, but centred on Hove was a now-destroyed group containing rich objects of faience, amber, bronze and shale. Who the occupants of these barrows were is uncertain, but clearly they had very high status; chiefs or priests perhaps? A drinking cup cut out of a solid block of amber and excavated from the Hove Barrow is on display in Brighton Museum.

Small farming communities living in the dry valleys on the Downs have left only sparse remains, with nothing visible on the land surface. They used bronze – as the discovery of bronze flat axes clearly shows – and by 1,000BC bronzesmiths were working throughout the county. Their axes, awls, neck and finger rings, pins and sickles are on show in museums throughout the region. Movement high on to the Downs around 1,000 BC has left traces of many farmsteads from the Later Bronze Age, including a well-excavated example at Black Patch, near Alciston. This shows exactly what life was like at the time and comprises a line of five round huts set in rectangular fields where barley, wheat and broad beans were grown. Cattle,

Carved-amber drinking cup on show at Brighton Museum

sheep and pigs were herded there too, and wild foods such as sloes, blackberries and hazelnuts were collected. Crafts included weaving, leather-, bone- and wood-working and pottery making. Examples of these farmsteads, showing on the surface of the Downs as banked enclosures with hut platforms, may be seen above Lewes at Itford Hill and on Plumpton Plain.

Age of hillforts
Dominating practically every South Downs hilltop are the remains of great earth-and-timber fortresses. Some of these began life as peaceful stock enclosures, but by the Iron Age (about 600 BC) all were established as links in an elaborate system defending fields, cattle and farmsteads on the surrounding land. Today the great banks and ditches at Cissbury and the Devil's Dyke remain as monuments to Iron Age craftspeople and traders. People lived in great round houses like the one reconstructed at Butser – near Petersfield – and farmed all over the Downs, leaving lynchetted fields which survive to the present day. A particularly well-preserved group of such fields can be seen on Bullock Down, at Beachy Head.

Replica roundhouse in Queen Elizabeth Country Park at the Bronze and Iron Age site of Butser Hill

It appears that most hillforts became disused in the 100 years before the Roman Conquest. Instead, a great and wealthy tribal centre developed in the Chichester area, defended by huge dykes that were miles long and can still be traced across great tracks of land north of the city. Excavations at the eastern end of the Chichester Dykes have produced coin moulds, indicating a mint and clearly suggesting a tribal capital of importance.

Wealthy farms sprang up along the foot of the Downs. One, excavated at Oving in West Sussex, has shown evidence of wide-ranging trade contacts, including amphorae of Italian wine – perhaps from the area around Pompeii and Herculaneum. High up on the Downs at sites like Park Brow, north of Worthing, poorer farmers continued to work in a Later Bronze Age fashion – but with expanding markets were able to sell their crop surpluses through the tribal centre. By 50 BC, or even before this, trade was increasingly with the Roman World.

Colony of Rome

Roman administration probably moved into Sussex partly by negotiation with pro-Roman native forces in the kingdom of *Verica*, with the result that there was less need for the legionary force required elsewhere in England. *Pax Romana* and the arrival of a few key individuals from the Roman Empire – administrators, traders, entrepreneurs and perhaps a few soldiers – stopped petty quarrelling between local aristocrats and diverted their energy into making Sussex part of the granary of Rome. This brought fabulous wealth to the successful few, some of whom built great houses at Fishbourne and Bignor – elaborate mosaics with patternbook designs in the Roman fashion survive – and at Arundel and Angmering. These great, 1st-century AD villas were centres of vast estates managing many smaller farms which had timber houses and have left little trace on the ground. Excavations beneath the surface north of Worthing at Park Brow have, however, revealed five rectangular

Model reminder of an illustrious Roman past in the District Museum, Chichester

Detail of a 1st-century Roman mosaic at Bignor villa

houses of timber. The walls of wattle and daub were plastered and painted in red, perhaps emulating those of rich men living in the great villas.

The 'native' Roman farmstead concentrated on the production of wheat, while bone evidence from a site near Beachy Head on Bullock Down indicates flocks of sheep. Wheat produced on such farms was marketed through the Roman town at Chichester. That town – perhaps developed from an Iron Age tribal capital – became a garrison at the Roman Conquest, as evidenced by large quantities of military equipment and house plans resembling military barracks found during excavations below Chapel Street. Political problems in the 2nd century AD led to the construction of the first of a series of town walls, remains of which can still be seen.

Religion was used by the Romans in their control of native populations, with local cults being encouraged and often Romanised. However, in Chichester evidence has been found of truly Roman religion, including an inscription recording the building in the 70s and 80s AD of a temple to Neptune and Minerva – with specific permission from the local King Cogidubnus. In the countryside high on the Downs were temples, constructed – using Roman techniques – to honour local deities. These Romano-Celtic institutions were square buildings within ditched temple precincts, as at Lancing. At Chanctonbury Ring, above Washington, the old Iron Age ramparts were used as the temple precinct, and a square temple was built within them.

If the South Downs region was part of the granary of Rome, then the claylands to the north were part of Rome's forge. During the occupation period the Weald became the major ironworking centre in Britain, supplying nails, picks, shovels, hammers and all manner of military and naval equipment to the Empire.

Saxon invasion

AD477. In this year AElle and his three sons Cymen, Wlencing and Cissa, came into Britain with three ships at a place called Cymenesora, and there killed many Britons and drove some into flight into the wood which is called Andredeslea.

In these words the *Anglo-Saxon Chronicle* describes the end of Roman Sussex and the beginning of Saxon rule. These invading Saxons left rich cemeteries at Selmeston, Alfriston, Bishopstone and elsewhere, from which gold, bronze and glass ornaments buried with the dead can be seen in museums at Worthing, Brighton and Lewes. Having taken control, the Saxons soon

Demonstration display of a Saxon burial, and examples of jewellery that might have accompanied the body. All exhibits are from the Barbican Museum, Lewes

church at Selsey, and by AD 1086 *Domesday* records over 100 more. Most were Saxon in origin and many Saxon building techniques – including long and short quoins, triangular headed windows and doors, and pilaster strips – can be seen in Sussex churches like those at Sompting and Worth.

With the development of kingship, the South Saxons became incorporated into the Kingdom of Wessex and finally under Alfred into the Kingdom of all the English. *Domesday* shows much about late-Saxon Sussex, recording 87 water-mills and showing extensive grinding of downland wheat for marketing through the rapidly developing towns at Steyning, Lewes, Hastings and Chichester. Coastal and riverine fisheries are also noted, as is large-scale salt production at 34 places. Remains of saltmaking sites survive as low mounds in the tidal estuary of the Adur.

Sompting's Saxon church has a gabled, pyramidal cap – known as a Rhenish helm – unique in England

merged with the local population and settled down to establish villages and farmsteads. All their houses were of timber, so little is left to see, but excavations on Bishopstone Hill have revealed a village of long timber houses. This clearly was planned, with houses neatly laid out in east-west alignments along the contours.

The economy of Saxon villages and farmsteads on the Downs returned very much to pre-Roman patterns. Sheep dominated, and remains of cattle, pig, horse, fowl and goose have been found at Bishopstone. The inhabitants of that coastal village also fished along the shoreline, and quern stones (for grinding corn) from a Saxon hut site at Old Erringham prove that crops were grown – although no fields have yet been found.

Christianity and a new nation

Although Christianity was an accepted Roman religion, all traces of it in Sussex were removed by the Saxons. Wilfrid effectively re-established Christianity in Sussex with the construction of a

HIC HAROLD·MARE·NAVIGAVIT·ETVE·LIS·VE NIT: VVTO COM

Pre-Conquest part of the Bayeux Tapestry showing the Saxon Duke Harold at Bosham before he sailed to Duke William of Normandy with the offer of England's crown

Norman Conquest

Sussex was probably one of the first parts of England to come under the direct control of a Norman lord. William the Conqueror successfully defeated King Harold on the grassy hills where Battle Abbey now stands. With him came Earl William de Warrene, who – as a loyal supporter – was given lands in Sussex, Surrey and Norfolk, whereupon he immediately set about building a castle at Lewes. This early-Norman stronghold was probably in the motte-and-bailey style, featuring a great earthen mound surrounded by a palisaded enclosure. On the motte, which still survives in the middle of Lewes as Brack Mount, was a wooden watch tower. Having rapidly consolidated his position, William de Warrene set about constructing a masonry castle, the remains of which can still be visited off the High Street in Lewes. Other castles were soon built at Bramber, Chichester, Hastings and Pevensey, all visible manifestations of a foreign power. The Norman lords and many of the monasteries founded by them in Sussex maintained direct links with France, and each main inland feudal town established an outpost to handle trade with that country – for instance, at Seaford, New Shoreham, Littlehampton and Winchelsea (see page 52). With strong central and local government, Sussex prospered in the 12th and 13th centuries AD. Between AD1200 and 1350, for example, at least 26 new fairs and markets were established, doubling the number prior to the Norman Conquest.

Medieval farmers

Although the dramatic remains of medieval Sussex survive as castles and churches, its wealth remained in farming, little trace of which survives today. A remarkable survival of ridge-and-furrow fields on Bullock Down, near Beachy Head, shows how the Downs were cultivated in strip fields. Excavations of the freeman's farmstead on Bullock Down have shown that it began in a small way about AD1250, with a single longhouse in which animals and people shared warmth under the same roof. By AD 1500 the farm had developed into a form that would be recognised today, with a farmyard enclosed by a farmhouse with hearth and chimney, two barns or byres and a couple of pig sties.

The economy of the Bullock Down farm, and indeed all farmsteads of the period established on the South Downs, was based on sheep-corn husbandry. Sheep were kept both for meat and, as spindle whorls for spinning show, for wool. Some cattle and pigs were kept for milk and meat, while remains of a few horses, cats and dogs indicate that such animals fulfilled the same role on a medieval farm as they do today. Seed remains from Bullock Down are evidence of wheat, barley and oats, while documents show that peas and beans were also grown. Over 18,000 limpet shells found by archaeologists on the medieval farm on Bullock Down suggest, perhaps, a particular liking for that traditional Sussex dish, limpet pie. Periwinkles, oysters and mussels were also eaten.

Many farmsteads on the Downs clustered around churches, leading to the development of villages. These, which had been evolving rapidly since the Late Saxon period, survive and in many cases preserve fine examples of vernacular architecture from the period.

The landscape

Towards the 16th century, great landowners in Sussex increasingly saw the value of sheep – particularly for their wool in international trade – and small downland farmsteads became deserted as the land was grazed over by thousands of sheep. This episode in the long development of the South Downs turned them into the great, rolling landscapes of springy turf beloved of 19th-century poets, but agricultural practices over the last 30 years have altered the character of the downland once again. Today's huge fields of arable crops, stretching as far as the eye can see, merely represent the latest chapter in the history of the Downs.

Medieval field system at Bullock Down, Beachy Head

Along the South Downs Way

To follow the crest of the Downs as it lifts, dips and winds far above the Weald is an exhilarating experience. People have walked the route for thousands of years, and remains of their settlements and burials from as far back as Neolithic times punctuate the journey. There are extensive views on either hand. Cowslips, orchids and round-headed rampion still grow on slopes inaccessible to the plough, while skylarks, wheatears and stone-chats survive and, west of the Arun, deer flourish.

Gilbert White in 1773 wrote a much-quoted sentence:

Though I have now travelled the Sussex-downs upwards of thirty years, yet I still investigate that chain of majestic mountains with fresh admiration year by year; and I think I see new beauties every time I traverse it.

He would find plenty to marvel at still.

The South Downs Way from Eastbourne to the Hampshire border became the first official long-distance bridleway in 1972. The Countryside Commission plans to extend the route to Winchester soon, but meanwhile it is clear for walkers and riders for the length of the Downs, from Eastbourne to Butser Hill. To ride all the way must be pleasurable for the rider – although the horse, like the walker, may find the flinty stretches hard going. It is also permissible to ride a push-bike along the way, but this is likely to appeal to the rough-stuff cyclo-cross enthusiast only. The walker may make the journey comfortably in a week, finding accommodation on the way, or – with companions and two cars – explore it section by section. There is scarce shelter from the sun, rain or wind (which are more intense on the hills than in the Weald), and the weather is no less changeable now than when William Cobbett – on his way to Singleton in 1823 – 'rode a foot pace, and got here wet to the skin', after having been assured by two turnip hoers that there would be no rain.

From Eastbourne to Alfriston the rider must take a northerly route, while the energetic walker may follow the coast and the Cuckmere River. From Alfriston to Butser the route is shared by rider and walker.

Eastbourne to Alfriston by footpath (11 miles)

The first South Downs Way sign is beside a refreshment kiosk beyond the end of the Eastbourne promenade. Take the path above the playing fields of Whitebread Hole to Beachy Head, then follow the cliff edge – but not too closely. The sea is steadily eating the chalk away, and it is impossible to predict where or when the next fall will be. Birling Gap offers welcome refreshment. Beyond are the Seven Sisters: Went Hill Brow, Baily's Brow, Flagstaff Point, Brass Point, Rough Brow, Short Brow and Haven Brow. Flat Hill does not count, for eight sisters would just not do. From Haven Brow there is a remarkable view of the meanders of the Cuckmere, short-circuited by the New Cut in 1846. The South Downs Way follows the east bank of the Cut, where bird-watchers may be observed in their hides. From the Country Park Centre at Exceat the Way goes through the edge of Friston Forest to Westdean, where the walls of a medieval dovecot stand among vestiges of the manor house, and on through Litlington to join the bridleway at Plonk Barn – now a fine house.

Eastbourne to Alfriston by bridleway (8 miles)

The bridleway alternative starts in Paradise Drive, climbing steeply by chalk track to the crest of Pashley Down, with views over Pevensey Levels. Beyond the A259 and the Downs Golf Club, the track leads on to Willingdon Hill, where carved stones from the bombed Eastbourne branch of

Wide views unfold from the Way alongside Devil's Dyke

Origins of the Long Man at Windover Hill are obscure

Barclays Bank act as waymarks. From there the Wealdway long-distance footpath heads north on its 80-mile course to the Thames at Gravesend, but the South Downs Way turns west and descends Bourne Hill. In Jevington the route turns right on the road and – if the call of the Eight Bells can be resisted – left past the church, with its Saxon tower, and on into woods where nightingales sing. The Way then continues north to Windover Hill, with a view of Wilmington and its medieval priory. Out of sight on the scarp below is the Long Man looking 'naked to the shires'. A wide path leads down to a sunken track and the road at Plonk Barn. Walkers and riders alike cross the wooden bridge to Alfriston. Here the South Downs Way crosses the Vanguard Way, a long-distance footpath from Seaford to Croydon.

Alfriston to Southease (7 miles)

The Way leaves Alfriston beside the Star Inn's tame lion – figurehead of a 17th-century Dutch man-of-war – climbing at first on a residential road and then along a chalk track to a long barrow. Subsequently, it follows the ridge above Alciston (where people still skip communally on Good Friday), and Charleston Farm – Bloomsbury's country seat, where every square inch of interior surface succumbed to the decorative urge of Duncan Grant and Vanessa Bell – an urge that overflowed into Berwick church near by. Bopeep Barn recalls the happy time when these hills were sheep-walks, and shepherds would lope across for a talk with the stranger. From Firle Beacon the South Downs wayfarer looks down upon the tower in Firle Park and across to the chalk outlier of Mount Caburn, thence to Lewes. After the radio masts of Beddingham Hill the Way descends to Itford Farm, with views of Newhaven Harbour to the south, and crosses the River Ouse to Southease and its round-towered church.

Southease to the Newmarket Inn (6 miles)

Walkers can avoid the noisy half a mile along the roadside verge to Rodmell by taking the west bank of the Ouse for a mile and turning along a footpath to Rodmell, where they will pass the other Bloomsbury outpost of Monk's House – home of Virginia and Leonard Woolf.

Chanctonbury's beech clump is visible for miles

Opposite the Abergavenny Arms the Way continues past the garage and farrier's forge, up Mill Lane, and at the top turns right. A long stretch of concrete track is a bore initially, but soon Kingston Hill recalls the opening of W H Hudson's *Nature in Downland* – that pellucid description of his pleasure on a hot, windy August day in 1899, in watching the clouds of thistle-down which 'rose up from the ground to fly towards and past me. It was as if these slight silvery objects were springing spontaneously into existence, as the heat opened and the wind lifted and bore them away'. Soon the Way follows Juggs Lane, the old track from Lewes to Brighton, but before reaching the top of Newmarket Hill turns away around the head of Cold Combe to descend to Newmarket Inn on the A27.

The Newmarket Inn to Pyecombe (8 miles)

North of the A27 the Way climbs the dip slope and turns sharp left on to the ridgeway from Lewes. Here it crosses Plumpton Plain, where a Bronze Age farmstead has been discovered on a spur just south of the ridge. From Ditchling Beacon, at 248m (813ft) the highest point in East Sussex, can be seen 294m (965ft), Leith Hill, the highest point in Surrey and 280m (919ft), Blackdown, the highest point in West Sussex. Chanctonbury Ring, that symbol of Sussex, then comes into view. At Keymer Post the Way passes into West Sussex. Wooden signposts become plentiful and concrete signs vanish. The Way turns sharp left before Jack and Jill, the Clayton windmills, then right by the golf course to Pyecombe where – despite a revival in the 1970s – the forge no longer makes the Pyecombe Hook by which shepherds in these parts once swore.

However, those who are interested can see its design incorporated in the church gate, or by visiting Worthing Museum find examples of the real thing.

Pyecombe to the A283 at Upper Beeding (7½ miles)

The Way crosses the A23 near the Plough Inn and traverses the neck of Newtimber Hill. In the middle of the farming hamlet of Saddlescombe stands a square, black, weather-boarded well-house, open on one side and crowned with a pyramidal slate roof. Within is a huge wooden treadmill on which a donkey once worked to hoist water from a deep well. The chalk is a valuable aquifer, and springs burst out below its scarp; but settlements on the chalk itself had to dig deep for their water. The Way climbs beside the steep combe of the Devil's Dyke and leaves the hotel, the car park and the hang-gliders to the right. It keeps to the ridge above Fulking, with splendid views across the Weald, then swings south of the crest and affords views over the Brighton conurbation to the sea. After the radio masts of Truleigh Hill comes Tottington Barn, rebuilt first as a house and again in the 1970s as a youth hostel. The Way runs parallel with the road to a junction, then descends as a grassy track with views of Lancing College Chapel to the left, Bramber Castle to the right and St Botolph's Church ahead. On the west side of the A283 the Society of Sussex Downsmen has installed a tap and horse trough.

The A283 at Upper Beeding to Washington (6½ miles)

A bridge across the River Adur leads to the abandoned medieval village of Botolphs. Here the Downs Link, a 30-mile bridleway to the North Downs Way – mostly along a disused railway line – is waymarked with the symbol of a bridge. The South Downs Way climbs Annington Hill with Steyning below and, to the left, the formidable ramparts of Cissbury. There, 2,000 years before the Iron Age fort was built, Neolithic people mined high-quality flint. Chanctonbury Ring, whose clump of trees is a landmark to all wanderers in the Weald, offers a splendid view. The Way descends and crosses the A24, but riders wishing to avoid the dual carriageway – and all those in search of the successor to the beer that Hilaire Belloc found in the Washington Inn and spent six pages of *The Four Men* praising – may make a diversion through the village.

A donkey was used to pump water at Saddlescombe

Washington to Amberley (6½ miles)

West of the A24 in Glaseby Lane there is a tap for wayfarers. Soon the Way climbs high above Storrington; south are Church, Blackpatch and Harrow Hills, with Neolithic flint mines in their Upper Chalk, followed by vast areas of ploughed downland with the 19th-century silhouette of Arundel Castle in the distance. North are Parham Park, Amberley Wild Brooks – that ancient wetland saved from draining and the plough by a public outcry – and Amberley village, with its Bishop's Castle. The Way descends beside the Chalk Pit Museum, where industrial locomotives are in steam during the season, and follows a dangerous stretch of main road to the Arun. Here is the start of another linking route with the North Downs Way – the Wey-South Path, which follows the line of the Wey and Arun Canal to Guildford.

Amberley to Cocking (11 miles)

Beyond the Arun trees are more plentiful. This is the land Hilaire Belloc praised in *The South Country*:

> *The great hills of the South Country*
> *They stand along the sea;*
> *And it's there walking in the high woods*
> *That I could wish to be . . .*

The Way turns right to Houghton, takes a track beside Combe Wood, crosses the A29 and passes along the south-western slope of Westburton Hill. Here it zigzags past two black barns to Toby's Stone, a memorial to James (Toby) Wentworth-Fitzwilliam: 'Here he lies where he longed to be'. On Bignor Hill Stane Street is crossed on its course from Chichester's east gate to London Bridge. The thatched buildings protecting the mosaics of a Roman villa can be seen just east of Bignor, at the foot of the Downs. Now the Way takes a short cut to Littleton Down. It passes to the right of Crown Tegleaze, at 255m (836ft) the highest point on the Sussex Downs. It is shrouded in trees, as is much

Looking eastwards along the Way near Cocking Down

ARUNDEL CASTLE, *in* SUSSEX.

Published according to Act of Parliament, by Alexr Hogg, Nº 16 Paternoster Row.

Arundel Castle around 1770, before its restoration

of the Way for the next few miles. At Hill Barn a tap has been set in a flint cairn 'in memory of Peter Wren aged 14 years. He loved the English countryside and walked the South Downs Way in the summer of 1978'.

Cocking to Harting Down (6½ miles)

From the A286 at Cocking the Way climbs steadily to Lynch Down, from which are extensive views to the North Downs and south to Bow Hill, Chichester Cathedral and farther west, the Isle of Wight. The Devil's Jumps, Bronze Age round barrows, have been cleared of scrub by the admirable Society of Sussex Downsmen and are once again a venerable sight. In Philliswood the Way takes a sharp turn to the right. Take care, for the signpost here seems curiously vulnerable. Those who miss the turn reach the Royal Oak in Hooksway in a mile. The Way zig-zags south of massive Beacon Hill, for there is no bridleway over it, but the energetic walker should not be deflected. From the top it is possible to observe the dip slopes of the hills to the north, and thus reconstruct the Wealden dome in the imagination. Riders can enjoy almost as good a view from Harting Downs: South Harting with its green copper spire is below; Butser – the destination – looms ahead, surmounted by a telecommunications tower.

Harting Down to Butser Hill (7 miles)

Between the B2141 and the B2146 the path rounds the hill below Up Park Tower, through a hanger called The Bosom. Then comes a muddy stretch of track between hedges to the Hampshire border, where the South Downs Way at present officially ends. Fortunately, the track goes on past Sunwood Farm, and a few South Downs Way signs point the route past Coulters Dean Farm and Dean Barn to a wide bridleway that traverses Queen Elizabeth Country Park in an elongated 'S',

Reconstruction of an Iron Age village at Butser

passing the Country Park Centre. Then it tunnels under the A3, passes a demonstration Iron Age farm and ascends 270m (888ft) at Butser. The Hampshire County Council arranges with a local farmer for the grass to be grazed by sheep, so here the walker can tread turf such as has seldom been seen since leaving the Seven Sisters. After Butser the nature of the hills changes, the long escarpment ends and the Weald is left behind. Butser is not only the highest of the South Downs, it is the last – a fitting place to end the journey.

Woodland and Downland Wildlife

Everyone has a favourite place in the country – somewhere to visit and remember with affection. Naturalists are no exception. The choice may vary with the time of the year: woodland in spring; the Downs in early summer; heathland in late summer; a coastal headland in autumn; or an estuary in winter. But Sussex, and particularly the region of the South Downs, is graced by such a range of top-quality habitats that a visitor need never be more than a cycle ride from any such special place. Little wonder that the area is a Mecca for weekend connoisseurs of wildlife.

Purple emperor, a treetop butterfly of oak woodland

People new to the Weald are often surprised at the amount of tree cover on the rolling land north of the Downs. A look back over Sussex from the steep scarp slope shows hedges and woods large and small as integral parts of the rural patchwork. They recede into the far distances, changing from green to hazy blue or purple, melting into the horizon. The soils of the Weald are clays and sands that are difficult to work, and over the years farming has made little impression.

Primeval forest

Blocks of ancient woodland – remnants of the original primeval forest which covered most of Britain over 5,000 years ago – have survived remarkably well, though it cannot be claimed that they have avoided the axe for all that time. Far from it; woodland has always been a valuable resource, carefully maintained, but traditional management up to the pre-war years actually improved these woods for wildlife. Rides were opened, clearings cut and the sun allowed to strike through the canopy. Since the war many old woods have fallen derelict or been block-felled, underplanted with conifers, or had their rides sprayed with herbicides.

Even in the best woods April can be a disappointing time, but when spring has arrived in the hedgerows, when blackthorn blossom is in bloom, go back among the trees. If the understorey has recently been coppiced, with hazel bushes cut to the stumps allowing light to flood through to the forest floor, then May will see the ground carpeted in a deep pile of vernal flowers. Among them will be primroses, wood anemones, dog violets, bluebells – family favourites remembered by grandparents, who lived in an age when coppicing was more widely practised.

Oak is the most widespread deciduous forest tree, and many fine woods have public footpaths through them. During the early summer such places resound to the clamour of birdsong coming from residents such as the song thrush and robin, and migrants like the blackcap and redstart. In damp, leafy corners where sallow bushes grow may be heard the nightingale, a retiring member of the thrush family that is still quite common in the South Downs area and is easy to locate, by day or night. The song is strong, melodic and mellow; no other bird can match it except, perhaps, the blackbird.

Woodland emperors

In the heart of summer begin to appear the woodland butterflies for which Sussex is nationally famous, including the silver-washed fritillary and white admiral – often together on bramble blossom. In silhouette they look gigantic, but are eclipsed by the most elusive and mysterious of all English butterflies, the purple emperor. This was once thought to be very rare, the crowning glory of many an old butterfly collection. In fact, it is known to occur at a low density throughout Sussex, wherever extensive old woodland still survives.

Quite unlike any other butterfly, it soars around the tallest trees, the males congregating around a 'master oak'. The female may cover miles of countryside, flying effortlessly from wood to wood in search of suitable sallow bushes on which to lay her eggs. The life history of this most famous butterfly was a mystery until 1758, when the legendary entomologist Moses Harris was given a curious slug-shaped caterpillar. He fed it on sallow leaves until it pupated. Then, three weeks later on the

Both male and female nightingales feed their young

White wood anenomes are often flushed with purple

evening of the 23 June, the unidentified chrysalis emerged: 'To my unspeakable joy,' wrote Harris, 'it produced the male purple emperor . . . one of the most beautiful flies in the universe . . .' and so surely it is.

Wealden woods such as The Mens and Ebernoe Common are memorable, but there are some interesting and exciting places on the Downs too. Of these, Kingley Vale (see page 47) has to be mentioned. Tucked away among the whalebacks of chalk, this fragment of yew forest may represent a lost page in the ecology of the Downs. Yew grows prolifically elsewhere too, and is known locally as the 'weed of the Downs' because it covers whole hillsides, but mature trees are now few. At Kingley Vale there are groves of multi-stemmed trees, deformed by centuries of snow and storm, drought and deluge. Around the huddled yews are oaks and ashes, draped with the creeping stems of wild clematis. Kingley is a strange place much visited by the Victorians, who enjoyed its brooding pre-Raphaelite charm. Very few animals eat yew, and it is also poisonous to most insects. Even in their primeval heyday, yew forests must have been silent places.

The woodland that once covered most of the Downs was cleared for sheep grazing, and over many centuries the grassland thus created has developed an exceptionally rich flora. Some 6,000 acres is still 'unimproved' grassland, composed of close-cropped grasses such as sheep's fescue, and supporting an incredibly varied community of low-growing herbs and brightly-coloured flowers. The rest of the Downs is woodland, arable and 'improved' grassland, sprayed with fertiliser and pesticides – highly productive, but poor in wildlife.

Over 2,000 acres of old downland has been lost since the war, about half due to the encroachment of scrub resulting from the reduction in grazing by sheep and rabbits. To allow any more to disappear would be a careless waste of an important ecological asset; fortunately, many of the finest remaining stretches are protected in some way, and both sheep and rabbits are at work again.

The downland summer

Open downland is at its best in June and July. To get the right impression, the observer should select a south-facing slope on a sunny day and sit down for a few minutes. The earth feels warm and dry. This is a specialised habitat for plants, requiring a tolerance of thin alkaline soils and the ability to withstand the heavy, constant grazing – yet each square foot of the sward contains a bewildering assortment of flowers that may exceed a comparable area from any field or meadow this side of the Alps. Some plants are recognised as indicators of ancient downland, and if present show that the area in question has probably not been seriously disturbed since the Iron Age. Felwort, horseshoe vetch, rockrose, milkwort and clustered bellflower are all classic downland species. Other interesting and attractive flowers claim the attention of anyone who sits on them – thyme and marjoram because of their scent, stemless and carline thistles because of their prickles.

Orchids and insects

The South Downs has its own special plant, round-headed rampion, which is found only in a very few places outside Sussex. Orchids are remarkably common too, and the region is one of the best for bee orchids, occasionally in their hundreds. Also, in some secret localities are rarities such as the tiny burnt-tip orchid and the early spider orchid.

South-facing chalk slopes face the full glare of the sun. The air is often heavy with the scent of flowers, and in such conditions it is difficult to feel any urgency in life. Yet, all around there is feverish activity and the droning of a thousand wings – a riot of insects, many very beautiful, ranging from carder-bees to cardinal beetles. On the grass stems can be seen several kinds of grasshoppers – including the largest British species, the wartbiter. Day-flying moths, the foresters and the burnets, bronze blue and bright scarlet, dance drunkenly among the trefoil stems. Butterflies appear in profusion.

Downland is the only place where clouds of blue butterflies are still to be seen, just as they were a century ago. There are seven species of blue in the south of England, and all of them occur on the Downs. The jewel among them is the Adonis blue, the

Bee orchids (right) thrive on chalk slopes, where the rare Adonis blue butterfly (below) is sometimes spotted amongst horseshoe vetch

Fulmars are among many species seen from Beachy Head

colour of a summer sky. The failing British climate
and loss of suitable habitat has made the Adonis a
rare creature, as much a glittering prize for
butterfly-watchers on the Downs as the purple
emperor is in woodland. Among the many other
Downs butterflies are the marbled white, a
chequered cream and chocolate relative of the
meadow brown, the chalk-hill blue (closely related
to the Adonis but silver-blue in colour) and the
dark green fritillary. Altogether about 30 species
occur in this habitat, representing half the British
check-list.

Wealden heaths

As the summer advances the attention of naturalists
is drawn back to the Weald, to areas of heathland
covered in heather. This type of habitat is in very
short supply, and even Sussex has only a few
fragments surviving. Iping and Amersham
Commons are the most important, with heaths
that are very ancient and vegetation that was
probably established 8,000 years ago – earlier than
other more famous places in Dorset and Surrey.
Populations of classic heathland birds and animals,
like the Dartford warbler and sand lizard, have
survived only precariously – but stonechats and
adders are quite numerous and much more likely
to be seen. This is also the sort of country for the
silver-studded blue butterfly and the tiger beetle;
the place to wait at dusk on a warm thundery
evening to hear the strange churring of nightjars
and the roding of woodcocks.

Migration plays an important part in the lives of
many animals. To be on the south coast when
insects or birds are on the move is an unforgettable
experience, although it is impossible to predict the
right wind and weather that will bring in long-
distance travellers. A southerly breeze can
sometimes herald the arrival of clouded-yellow
butterflies and convolvulus hawk-moths. Bird
migration can be very noticeable at times, with
days in autumn when the bushes in combes and
valleys are alive with garden warblers and redstarts,
perhaps among them more distant or unusual
wanderers such as melodious warblers and
wrynecks.

Along the shore

The waifs and strays do not stay for very long, and
move on as quickly as they can, en route from
Europe to Africa. Seawatching from Beachy Head
has become a popular pastime for serious 'birders'.
Stiff gales bring seabirds close inshore, within
telescope range of the cliffs, and there are now
regular reports of Pomarine skuas, Balearic

Pagham Harbour Nature Reserve is known for wildfowl

shearwaters and Sabine's gulls – not to mention
the regular coastal fare of fulmars, divers, Arctic
skuas and kittiwakes.

The exciting variety of wildlife in and around the
South Downs is no better illustrated than in the
changing focus from woods to hills, from heath to
sea cliffs. However, in the winter many habitats
seem to be deserted; the flowers have been frosted,
next year's butterflies are hibernating as larvae or
pupae in the leaf litter, and most birds have moved
south. At this time the best places to be are the
flooded fields of Amberley Wild Brooks –
sometimes the refuge of large numbers of wigeon
and teal – and the harbours at Pagham and
Chichester.

Sheltered waters are always in demand by
overwintering birds, especially if there is a ready
supply of food at hand. The tideline attracts
waders, black-tailed godwits and grey plovers, as
well as abundant dunlins. Among the wildfowl are
Brent geese and pintails, goldeneyes and
mergansers. The specialities of the harbours in
winter are the small grebes, the black-necked and
the Slavonian, half the size of the great-crested and
at least twice as difficult to see, even on a still day.

No matter how impressive the coastal wildlife of
Sussex is in winter it is impossible to conclude any
summary of the area without referring back to
summer – just as it is impossible while walking the
shore not to glance north to the hills. Surely
nowhere in England can be closer to the heart of
the country. Dappled oakwoods, and Downs
spangled with a thousand flowers; such memories
are worth an occasional long weekend.

Traditional Local Buildings

One of the richest and most varied concentrations of traditional building in Britain survives in a region comprising the South Downs, the coastal plain to the south, and a few miles of country lying north of the inland escarpment. A glance at the geological map of the area reveals why. The chalk of the Downs is dominant, but immediately to the north and south run other strata of sandstone, limestone and various forms of clay. Until recent times cottages and farm buildings – even churches and manor houses – were built from materials found in the immediate locality, a practice which gave particular character to the villages and farmsteads on the different geological beds. Even the type of timber used varied according to its source, with oak characteristic of the Weald, and elm – now depleted by disease – of the coastal plain. Also, bricks and tiles from the gault and Weald clay in the north differ in colour and texture from those of the clay deposits in the south.

Flint and chalk

Within the area of the Downs, from earliest times to the 19th century, flint and chalk were the principal building materials. Flint was used for exteriors, and chalk for interior walls and partitions. Both were employed widely by the Romans for everything from villas to temples, as has been shown on sites at Highdown, above Worthing; Chilgrove, near Chichester; Chanctonbury Hill; and Bow Hill. Later, the Normans used flint for churches, manor houses and castles such as those at Bramber and Arundel. Excavations on the site of Hangleton village, which

Vernacular architecture in the Downs region reflects the nature of the underlying rocks – chalk and flint, clays, plus various sandstones and limestones

was deserted in the 14th and 15th centuries, have revealed buildings mostly of flint rubble, with occasional timber reinforcement. This method of construction was probably typical of most of the villages and farmsteads built on the Downs during the Middle Ages. In the valleys, however, timber-framing from the 14th and 15th centuries survives, often completely enclosed in skins of flint or brick added in the 17th or 18th centuries, and sometimes with a simple façade of those materials. Such changes might well have been made when an original central hall, open to the roof and with a hearth stone, gave way to the partition walls, inglenooks and ceilings of the Tudor and Stuart periods.

Of farm buildings, only a few barns survive from before the 16th century; most were replaced or rebuilt in the 17th and 18th centuries. The majority are of flint, but a few – particularly the greater aisled barns – are of timber covered with weatherboard. Small timber farm buildings such as granaries on staddles (mushroom-shaped supporting stones) and cattlesheds are rapidly disappearing. Dovecotes surviving from the 15th century and later are usually round or square in plan, with flint exterior surfaces and chalk interior nesting boxes. A good one can be seen at Patcham, and a fine square example on the Downs above Shoreham has recently been saved from destruction by being incorporated into a new estate for future communal use.

Ruins of a medieval dovecote, near Alciston's church

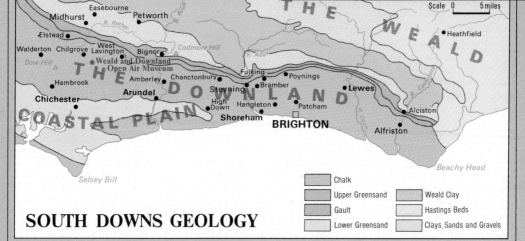

SOUTH DOWNS GEOLOGY

	Chalk
Upper Greensand	Weald Clay
Gault	Hastings Beds
Lower Greensand	Clays, Sands and Gravels

Naming local stone

There are many local names for the different types of stone used in the region: clunch is the hard chalk rock which occurs in shallow beds within softer material; malm stone is a hard limestone which outcrops from beneath the chalk on its north escarpment, providing a well-drained shelf along which springs of water and villages are strung from Alciston to Poynings in the east and from Fulking to Elstead in the west. Ragstone is a term rather indiscriminately used to describe various colours and textures of sandstones from the greensand belt. In the Weald clay is found ripple stone – a yellow sandstone used particularly for paving. Occasionally a hard limestone, full of fossil shells and known as Sussex marble, is used for interior ornamental stonework such as fire surrounds. Very attractive when polished, it has local names such as winkle stone, Petworth marble, Bethersden marble and Kirdford marble.

Flint has been used in a variety of applications, ranging from uncoursed and unshaped rubble walls, to ornamental work where the stone has been finely knapped, squared and laid in regular courses. Occasionally it appears with other materials in similarly decorative surface patterning – usually in churches and public buildings. A good example is the Marlipins at New Shoreham, the 13th-century façade of which was added to an earlier Norman building and displays a chequerboard pattern in which squares filled with the dark, broken textures of knapped flint alternate with single panels of grey Caen stone. After 600 years the contrast and definition remain little reduced by weathering or urban grime. Chequerboard of this kind was revived in the restoration of many churches in the 19th century, and for new secular buildings such as gatehouses. The Victorian lodge gates at West Lavington are a good example. Another form of flint decoration is galleting, in which the mortar joints in outer walls were filled with flint chippings. This is a technique particularly widespread in the western part of the Downs behind Chichester, and 18th-century examples survive on the Goodwood Estate. It is said that the practice was introduced to

Flint and stone chequering at the Marlipins, Shoreham

protect the mortar from weathering, but its purpose is likely to have been mainly decorative and dictated by fashion. The most spectacular example of galleting and knapped flint work is perhaps in the extensions to West Dean House – now West Dean College – which dates from the 1860s.

A form of decorative flint work seen from the lower downland slopes to the coast, uses carefully matched cobbles or beach pebbles for coursed work which has a regularity and precision which can only be appreciated by anyone who has attempted to built a flint wall. The degree of skill with which these techniques have been applied to so many cottages and humbler houses in the district is surprising – though usually it is only the façade, the public aspect of the building, that was so treated.

Limestone and the clay

North of the Downs, where the greensand belt extends for two or three miles from the escarpment to the flatter area of the Weald clay, is a different world. The acid soils support a different ecology, a different pattern of agriculture and, until the present century, fostered different building traditions. Within a few miles of the downland summits are the grey limestones of the upper greensand; the heavy gault clay, largely unbuilt on; and the red and brown sandstones of the Folkstone, Sandgate and Hythe beds. Greater variety, both in the natural landscape and in the farmsteads, villages and towns upon it, is found in this short distance than in the entire chalk Downs.

Up to this century stone from the upper greensand and bricks made in the many brickyards dotted along the gault clay, were the main building materials. From Tudor times to the end of the 19th century almost every parish had its own small brick-field, where bricks were made when the need arose. However, the coming of easy and cheap transport concentrated production into a relatively few well-situated and efficient large-scale brickyards, which operated permanent kilns instead of temporary clamps. Despite the spread of this material, there still remain under the escarpment of the Downs villages in which most of the buildings – including the church, the manor house and even the Victorian school – were built of materials from the immediate locality. They preserve characteristics entirely different from the flint villages of the Downs or those on the sandstone of the lower greensand belt, a mile or two to the north. Any flint used here is usually seen near a river, along which it would have been transported.

Between the gault clay and the Weald clay are various strata of lower greensand which provide building stone ranging in colour from light to deepest brown. The stone is quarried locally, and in some cases it is possible to identify a farmyard pond as the pit from which the farmhouse and most of the farm buildings came. Few of these quarries survive. The best and probably most accessible is at Easebourne, near Midhurst, and one of the largest at Codmore Hill, near Pulborough, now cleared of trees and undergrowth; the latter has a rock face sufficiently high to challenge climbers. Most of Midhurst and Pulborough, including their churches, can be said to have been built from these quarries.

Market towns

There are a few places where all the region's local building traditions are brought together – the market towns standing on rivers which cut through the Downs from north to south, providing relatively easy transport routes. These are Lewes and Alfriston in East Sussex, Steyning and Arundel in West Sussex and, to a lesser extent, Petworth and Midhurst. In old 'focal points' such as these are found many examples of oak timber-framing, typical of the Wealden area of Surrey, Sussex and Kent, side-by-side with cobble flint brought up from the coast – and in some larger houses and churches, Caen stone from across the Channel. Such mixtures of materials reflect a wider community.

Timber-framed building attracts the eye more than any other, since the structures in which it is

Timber-framed Anne of Cleves' House, in Lewes

used are clearly defined and the infill of plaster or brick within the wooden framework provides interesting patterning and contrasting colour. This decorative effect was often deliberately elaborated, though not to the same extent here as in parts of East Anglia or in the West Country. Examples of timber-framed buildings open to the public and worth visiting include Anne of Cleves' house in Lewes, the County Library in Midhurst (converted from two terraced Tudor cottages) and in particular the Clergy House adjacent to Alfriston church. The last-mentioned is one of the earliest surviving examples of a medieval Wealden house, so called because it occurs most abundantly in the central Weald. In such buildings the open hall is flanked by jettied upper storeys on either side and recessed, but the whole of the front is under a continuous roof. On the downland chalk this type of dwelling is scarce, but many survive immediately to the north and five have been identified in Steyning – though much transformed. Possibly the best-preserved and certainly the most-photographed example is the Old Shop at Bignor. Nearly a century later than Alfriston's Clergy House, it has an infill of brick and flint instead of wattle and daub and represents the close of the medieval open-hall tradition. The hall itself is relatively small.

Distinctive roofscape formed by the variety of buildings in Steyning

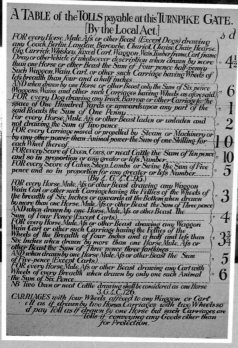

Flint-and-brick cottage and (left) a relic of turnpike days, both at the Weald and Downland Museum

Many timber-framed structures lost their identity behind new fronts built during and since the Tudor period, escaping notice when – under the 1949 Town and Country Planning Act – buildings of historic or architectural interest were listed. Also, within the last 200 years camouflaging quite different from the brick or flint façades usual in the 17th and 18th centuries has replaced the first 'disguises'. For instance, stucco has given a uniform appearance to buildings of stone, flint, brick or timber. It and its fashionable Regency associations spread out from developing Brighton, often accompanied by the raising of the front of the building to form a parapet which effectively hid the roof as seen from ground level. Such masking is not easy to detect, except from the side or rear of the structure.

On the roofs
One external feature more subject to alteration than even the walls is the roof covering. A common assumption is that in rural areas thatch was normal, but when the deserted medieval village of Hangleton was excavated there were found several cottages and farmsteads that had boasted tile roofs of Cornish slate, brought in by sea. Although brick making and brick building in the region dates from the 16th century, tile making for flooring, walling and roofing was general throughout the Middle Ages wherever good clay could be found. Today, thatch is to be found here and there, and its use has been revived in villages such as Amberley. However, the only area where it has been and remains a continuing tradition is on the coastal plain south of Chichester – a long-established corn-growing area in which the use of thatch is linked more with the character of farming than anything else. Reed thatching was probably widespread in riverside districts, but the material survives in its original usage only as a base for internal plastering – although bought-in Norfolk or Devon reed is nowadays much in demand for roofing and re-roofing.

North of the Downs is found a roofing material

peculiar to the Wealden area – a very hard, laminated sandstone sometimes called Horsham stone. This is split into tiles and used in courses, with very large slabs weighing up to half a hundredweight each at eaves level and relatively small tiles just below the ridge. Many churches have Horsham-slab roofs, and in Steyning they are almost as much in evidence on the older houses as is clay tiling and thatch. The technique was widely applied and is seen on buildings ranging from cottages and quite small farm buildings to great mansions. Unfortunately, there are now no quarries providing the stone, and few tilers who know how to use it. The weight of the tiles, which were often secured by single oak pegs, made a low roof pitch necessary to prevent slipping. Many have been ousted by clay replacements, since even the massive oak rafters and cleft oak battens used to support them can eventually twist and give under the strain.

Weald and Downland Museum
At Singleton, near Chichester, is the Weald and Downland Open Air Museum (see page 69). Situated in the heart of the Downs, it reflects and illustrates some of the styles and changes in the building traditions of the area. There are, for example, reconstructions of a cottage from the medieval village at Hangleton and a medieval timber-framed house with an open hall from the village of Walderton, illustrating the way in which early buildings became enclosed in walls of flint and brick during the 17th century. An early brick building has been 'transplanted' from Lavant and a barn from the dip-slope of the Downs at Hambrook. There are also a water-mill built of lower greensand stone galetted with iron-stone chippings, two examples of Horsham-slab roofing and a weatherboarded toll cottage from Beeding complete with toll-board and gate.

Combined with tours of the hamlets, villages and towns that are so individually distinctive of the region's multi-faceted character, a visit to the museum will give a greater depth of understanding through which the complex building traditions of the Downs and their adjacent areas can be fully appreciated.

Gardens of the Downs and Weald

In an area of relatively limited size, the South Downs region contains a remarkable selection of fine gardens, several of which qualify for that much abused adjective 'great'. It is impossible to quantify, but great gardens have an almost indefinable 'extra' which is invariably recognised and appreciated by all visitors, no matter what their level of expertise.

Why do the gardens of the Downs contain so many delights? To a small degree the answer 'lies in the soil', but it is largely because a number of wealthy and talented amateur gardeners chose to make their homes and gardens there. This happened particularly in the last century and coincided with a revival period of garden design – due largely to the influence of William Robinson and Gertrude Jekyll. Both called for a return to the 'natural' garden and, although they were designing mostly for the large country house, their ideas were adopted by owners of smaller houses which eventually became homes for professional people.

The plant hunters

The founding of the Royal Horticultural Society in the early 1800s had stimulated the development of interest in plants. Inevitably, the Victorians – with their great passion for travelling – initiated a series of expeditions which were to discover and introduce to the West a whole new range of plants from areas like the Andes, the Himalayas and China. One of the best-known plant collectors, Sir Joseph Hooker, returned from his 1850 trip to the Himalayas with no fewer than 43 new species of rhododendron!

Many of the imported species proved particularly suitable for planting in the large clumps which were featured in the new-style gardens. Even more significantly, they adapted well to the comparatively poor soils of the South Downs ridge and, once established, required the attentions of fewer gardeners than did the older, more formal plantings. Perhaps best of all, many of them – particularly the ubiquitous rhododendron – hybridised well, allowing garden owners to develop individual strains. Interest in hybridisation had begun early in the 18th century, but it was not until the early years of the 19th that widespread research and the publishing of results led to a massive growth in the subject.

Most of the gardens established in the course of the last 100 or so years – either on the chalk Downs or the adjoining Wealden clays – have produced their own distinct and famous hybrids. But whether raising new species or not, the gardens in this area have invariably contributed to the history of gardening and given unfailing pleasure to visitors.

Highdown hybrids

Perhaps one of the best examples of a 'typical' Downs garden is Highdown. Begun in the early years of this century by a true amateur on a most

Beautiful Highdown Garden is famed for its hybrids

unpromising site, it is famous for at least one of its hybrids and for the profusion of its flora – including some species which no professional plantsman would have been foolish enough to include. Highdown sits on, or rather in, the uncompromising chalk slope of Highdown Hill, facing Ferring. Its major feature is an old chalk quarry planted in an apparently haphazard fashion with a variety of plants and trees, many from mild climates. In early spring, when March winds blow, only an optimist would call the climate mild; yet, as a result of good husbandry – begun by owners Sir Frederick and Lady Stern and continued by Worthing Corporation – everything thrives. From the quarry, the ground rises to a rose garden before declining to follow the south-facing slope of the hill.

Here are more formal beds in which Sir Frederick grew most of the hybrids for which he became famous, although the best-known – *Magnolia Highdownensis* – grows in the quarry. From the flowering of the earliest Lenten Rose (*Helleborus Orientalis*) to the last rose of autumn, Highdown is a living and delightful memorial to its builders – to whom there is a small plaque beside one of the pools in the quarry, their finest achievement.

Genius at West Dean
If the Sterns were mildly eccentric in a peculiarly English way, starting a garden where no garden could grow, Edward James was decidedly eccentric – and possibly a genius. West Dean Gardens may share a situation on the Downs with Highdown, but little else. It is on an altogether larger scale, with massive trees – some pre-dating the James Wyatt Gothic house begun in 1804 – as the most obvious feature. A garden has existed on the site since the earliest years of the 17th century, and several of the trees are among the finest representatives of their species in Britain.

Several styles can be observed in the garden – the 19th-century passion for creating arboreta, which Edward James's father William grafted on to the existing parkland; Edward James's own earlier plantings, in similar vein; clear indications of early 20th-century 'romantic', with a fascinating knapped-flint and horse's-teeth gazebo among several other edifices. Edward James was very interested in arts and crafts, and the curriculum of the college which now occupies the house reflects this interest – as does the nearby Weald and Downland Open Air Museum, whose site was provided by him. There is some interesting modern shrub planting and, within the Victorian glasshouses in the walled garden, an exhibition of garden history. For connoisseurs of classic trees, nearby St Roche's Arboretum, in the same ownership (the Edward James Foundation) possesses some even more outstanding specimens, particularly of conifers.

Gardens on the clay
Two more gardens physically close on the Wealden clay are Borde Hill and Heaselands but, unlike West Dean and St Roche's, they are very different in scale and design. Relatively small, Heaselands was developed in two main phases – during the 1930s when a series of trees was planted to provide long-term shelter for the hilltop site, and in the 1950s, when the bulk of the shrub planting was carried out by owner Ernest Kleinwort. In fewer than 30 acres Mr Kleinwort managed to create a

Leonardslee, always lovely, excels in late spring

comprehensive selection including small rock, rose, wild and woodland gardens and – linking the whole – a water garden produced by the damming of a small stream to create a series of lake-like ponds on which a fine collection of wildfowl is maintained.

Borde Hill is larger in scale – literally 10 times the size of Heaselands. The Stephenson Clarke family have owned Borde Hill since the late 19th century, and three generations have contributed to the development of one of the finest gardens still in private hands. Carefully laid out, but with an air of informality, the basic design owes much to the first owner, who used the contours of the land to great effect, enticing the visitor along grassy paths to discover a truly remarkable selection of plants. Many of the species were collected in the 1920s, when a revival of interest in plant-hunting expeditions resulted in a great variety of new species. An expedition to Bhutan in the mid 1980s added to the rhododendron collection, in which all the Stephenson Clarke family have taken great interest. A whole day should be set aside for this garden.

The expansiveness and style of Borde Hill is combined with the charm of the Heaselands water garden at Leonardslee, which should also be savoured at leisure. For a few days each spring Leonardslee comes as close to perfection as any garden in England. This is not to suggest that it is not worth visiting for the rest of the year, simply that a magical combination of weather and nature seems to produce a mixture of colours and scents which are unsurpassed but fleeting. It is possible to visit Leonardslee on a Thursday leaving at closing time with senses reeling only to return on Sunday to find a subtle, almost indefinable change. For the rest of the spring season the garden reverts to being simply one of the very best – equalling the great spring gardens of the south-west of England.

No one who has ever visited Leonardslee will forget the views – a cunning blend of nature and man – which contain more than a hint of a mythical land, stretching away to the horizon. At the bottom of the steep valley sides, the carefully extended hammer ponds reflect the rich colours of azaleas and rhododendrons, and the Oriental

Water gardens at the part-Elizabethan Wakehurst Place

Magnolia Campbellii grows in a wooded Wakehurst dell

beauty of Japanese Maple, *Acer palmatum*. The Loder family have now owned Leonardslee for 100 years, and it is 80 years since their most famous cross *Rhododendron* 'Loderei' made its first appearance. All who have bought this splendid plant or visited the garden have reason to be grateful for their stewardship.

Spanning three centuries
Stewardship of a different kind, that of the National Trust, has maintained Sheffield Park at the forefront of the great gardens of the world. If the site at Leonardslee lent itself naturally to the creation of a fine woodland garden, then Sheffield had the accoutrements of a classic garden long before Mr Arthur Soames acquired it in 1909. Indeed, Sheffield *is* the history of 300 years of gardening – century overlaid on century, but each still clearly discernible.

As at West Dean, there is a Gothic house by Wyatt (much changed, and not for the better) and a park landscape designed by 'Capability' Brown, containing his standard layout of trees, lawns and serpentine lakes. All this was provided by the 1st Lord Sheffield, and over the next 100 years a rock garden and two more lakes were added, softening and drawing together the strands of Brown's design. To this Mr Soames added an outstanding collection of plants, distributed with an unerring instinct for dramatic effect and good taste. In a sense, this is best appreciated out of season, when

– lacking the famous riot of spring or autumn colour – the outlines of trees and shrubs are aesthetically satisfying, perfectly mirrored on the surface of the lakes.

Since the death of Mr Soames in 1948, the fame of Sheffield Park has continued to grow, and it is now one of the most visited, most photographed, most written about gardens in Britain.

The National Trust also owns Wakehurst Place (which is leased to the Royal Botanic Gardens, Kew) and Nymans. Superficially there are similarities between the gardens, but Wakehurst is the larger and has more in common with Sheffield Park. Gerald Loder (later Lord Wakehurst), was the driving force behind the early 20th-century planting of the quite breathtaking variety of species at Wakehurst, which is a garden of progressions.

Around the house, still in part Elizabethan, are formal gardens and island beds which transpose into a delightful area of pond and rock gardens, water gardens and a little valley complete with stream. Dwarf conifers, exotics, bog plants, masses of magnolias and delicate leaved *Acers* are planted in this relatively small area. Elsewhere the character changes as paths plunge into a large valley filled with native and introduced trees, underplanted with a wonderful collection of rhododendrons, highlighted by a beautiful *Magnolia campbellii* and a fine dove (or handkerchief) tree, *Davidia involucrata vilmoriniana*. At the foot of the valley is a large lake, then more delights as paths wander through spring woods and conifer plantations.

Easy to explore
Sadly, much of Wakehurst is not easily reached by the infirm or disabled, but Nymans is much more accessible. This is a family garden of some 30 acres, started by Ludwig Messel in the 1890s and

Camellias, a feature of Nymans, surround the dovecote

dovecot and tithe barn; and the garden is full of roses. The garden, designed by the painter Sir Oswald Birley and his wife, is full of visual delights. Started in the 1930s, it reflects the still-strong influence of Gertrude Jekyll and includes a series of small, cottage-style enclosures, including a walled kitchen garden and a charming orchard.

Coates is another garden which reflects the owner's artistic ability. Mrs G H Thorp was a flower arranger, and form is – not surprisingly – of great importance in her garden, which is not yet 30 years old. Entirely her own creation from an unpromising site, it features three distinct areas – a lawn, with shrubs; a garden with emphasis on trees; and a charming small walled section. Many of the trees are represented by a single specimen, underplanted or set off by clumps of carefully-chosen plants, often with a particular colour theme.

A few miles to the south is the third of the trio, Denmans, another post-war garden with an emphasis on overall effect of both shape and colour. The aim of owner Mrs J H Robinson was to create an easily-managed garden providing year-round interest. Winter flowers give way to masses of summer plants under trees chosen for their foliage, the whole enclosed by old climber-covered walls.

The great estates

This short survey has necessarily ignored the great downland houses of Uppark, Goodwood, Parham and Petworth. Gardens may not be their strongest feature – although the four-acre walled garden at Parham is a fine example of the work of modern designer Peter Coates – but their parks are historically important and from them have evolved the sort of gardens we now prize. Then there are the many other fine gardens which are opened each year by their owners under the aegis of the National Gardens Scheme (see page 77). Often on a smaller scale, perhaps concentrating on a single species or specific natural feature, they too give great pleasure.

'Dreamer' is one of several contemporary works by Marion Smith exhibited at Denmans

enlarged by succeeding members of his family. Part of its enduring charm is the impression it conveys of being not quite designed! It comprises a series of small gardens, based on the ideas of William Robinson and Gertrude Jekyll, but instead of each keeping strictly to its own place, sections run into each other in the most delightful way. Plants, particularly trees, often appear to be in the wrong place – presumably, once they were established no one had the heart to move them. In short, Nymans is loved because it resembles 'home' gardens; not exactly what was planned. Just how much of this is artifice would make an interesting thesis.

Three small gardens on or near the Downs are Charleston Manor, Coates Manor and Denmans. There can be few more romantic sites than Charleston. It lies in a lovely, sheltered valley; the house has been described as 'perfect'; there is a

SOUTH DOWNS

Gazetteer

Each entry in this Gazetteer has the atlas
page number on which the place can be
found and its grid reference included
under the heading.
An explanation of how to use the grid is
given on page 80.

*Above: the Long Man – cut in to the north face
of Windover Hill, near Wilmington – was designed
to be seen from a distance and is foreshortened
when seen close to. Maybe dating as far back as
Anglo-Saxon times, it was restored in 1874*

Alciston

Map Ref: 87TQ5005

Situated under the north side of the Downs, this little hamlet became known as the forgotten village after its population fled before the ravages of the Black Death, leaving a 13th-century church and 14th-century Alciston Court. The court – now a farmhouse – was once lived in by monks, and relics of ecclesiastical architecture are still to be found in the kitchen. Also in the village is a 170ft tithe barn, said to be the longest in the country, plus a duck pond and a street of neatly thatched and timbered cottages. On Good Friday traditional village skipping still takes place at the popular Rose Cottage pub.

The surrounding fields were once owned by the monks and have been cultivated for centuries. In the field near the church is a medieval dovecote, which in the winters of the Middle Ages provided a valuable source of meat. At the end of the lane – a few yards into the woods – is a narrow grass cross roads where horse-drawn coaches ran between Alfriston and Firle.

Alfriston

Map Ref: 87TQ5103

In 1405 Henry IV gave 'The King's Town of Alfryston' the right to hold a weekly market and twice-yearly fair. Today visitors still flock to this picture-book and one-time smuggling village which stands three miles inland from Seaford. It has a street lined with medieval timber-framed houses, flint cottages with overhanging tiles, the stump of an

Alfriston's main street widens into a triangle where the market cross – the only one left in East Sussex – stands

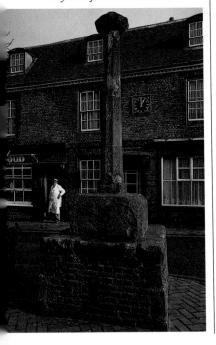

Although prairie farming has destroyed many species of downland flowers, the field edges still support a rich variety

old market cross and a spreading chestnut tree in the small square.

The old Smugglers Inn has six staircases, 21 rooms and 48 doors, and was once the home of smuggler and local butcher Stanton Collins. It now welcomes walkers, many crossing the village on the South Downs Way – though they are asked to leave their boots at the door! The half-timbered George Inn has had an innkeeper's licence since 1397, and the 500-year-old Star opposite was used by pilgrims on their way to and from Chichester.

Across the village green (known as The Tye) is 14th-century timber-framed and thatched Clergy House, which was built for parish priests in Chaucer's time and in 1891 became the first National Trust property – for £10. In a curve on the river is the beautiful 14th-century church of St Andrew's, standing in a circular graveyard. Known as the Cathedral of the South Downs, it was built in the form of a Greek cross with a central tower and shingled spire. Inside is a marriage register – one of the oldest in England – that dates from 1504. Medieval murals were recently discovered by decorators repairing the walls.

About a mile from the village near the A27 Lewes–Eastbourne road is Drusillas Zoo Park, known as the best small zoo in the south. Attractions include over 400 animals and birds; an oak-beamed and thatched barn restaurant; a pub serving real ale and English wines; a cottage bakery; a Japanese garden; and pottery, leather and garden shops. Near by is The English Wine Centre, with its wine museum, vine garden, and guided tours.

Across the Cuckmere River at Lullington is a very tiny church – only 16ft square, and with no more than 20 seats inside. It cannot really claim to be the smallest church in the country because it is no more than a chancel. Built of rough flints and stone, with a white weather-boarded belfry, it is the remains of a much larger building that belonged to Battle Abbey. St Richard of Chichester installed a vicar at Lullington in the 14th century, and services are still held there on the first Sunday of the month.

AA recommends:
Hotels: Deans Place, 3-star, *tel.* (0323) 870248
Star, 3-star, *tel.* (0323) 870495
Restaurant: Moonraker's, High St, 1-fork, *tel.* (0323) 870472
Guesthouse: Pleasant Rise (farmhouse), *tel.* (0323) 870545

Amberley

Map Ref: 85TQ0213

Mercifully secluded on a side road off the B2139, this exceptionally pretty village consists entirely of old stone, flint and half-timbered dwellings standing in old-fashioned cottage gardens. The only sign of 'industrial' activity is a craft centre installed in a disused chapel. One of several small lanes leads to the 12th- and 13th-century Church of St Michael, which has an old castle towering above it, and becomes a footpath to Amberley Wild Brooks. These water meadows are protected wildfowl habitats.

In the church is a fine 15th-century brass effigy of John Wantele, and the castle was originally one of the three manor houses owned in the Middle Ages by the Bishops of Chichester.

Amberley Chalk Pits Museum is an open-air exhibition of industrial archaeology occupying a 36-acre site and displaying the memorabilia of industry in south-east England. Situated next to Amberley Station, the site was a chalk pit and limeworks for over 100 years until the 1960s. The whole process of lime production is the subject of a display, and elsewhere a blacksmith, printer, potter and boat-builder work with traditional tools and machinery in their own workshops, which are open to public view. Part of the industrial narrow-gauge railway exhibit is a workman's train on which visitors can ride – but which has deliberately been left as uncomfortable as it was when in regular use. There is a large collection of steam road transport too, and a Southdown 1920s bus section offers rides.

AA recommends:
Restaurant: Quins, Houghton Bridge, 1-fork, *tel.* (079881) 790. (1m S of village).

Ardingly

Map Ref: 86TQ3429

Ardingly (pronounced Ardingl-eye) is a scattered but fairly unspoilt village, with a public school one mile to the south and a delightful 189-acre reservoir with a sailing school and fishing with fly or float. Half a mile west is an ancient church, and a mile north is Wakehurst Place – built by Sir Edward Culpeper at the end of the 16th century. In the heart of the

Crafts, industry and industrial memorabilia are demonstrated and displayed at Amberley Chalk Pits

village, part of which used to be called Hapstead Green, is a pretty High Street with an hotel and old pub – both of which are busy when Ardingly is home to the South of England Show each June.

Wakehurst Place was left to the National Trust by Sir Henry Price in 1963, and two years later the

house and 500 acres were leased to the Royal Botanic Gardens at Kew. Today the garden is one of the few to be open to the public every day of the year except New Year's Day and Christmas Day (see page 29). For those interested in rare plants, birds and woodland animals, there is a 100-acre nature reserve – but access is a mile from the nearest car park. Numbers of visitors are limited and a special permit is needed to go there.

Inside the house is an exhibition covering the geology, habitats and woodlands of the area.

Stoolball–A Local Tradition

O ver 500 years ago the milk-maids of Sussex invented a game played with their three-legged milking stools and a ball. Not unnaturally, this became known as stoolball, and is considered by some to be the fore-runner of cricket. A proof offered in support of this is that the modern game has the same number of wickets as a milking stool has legs. Indeed, it is sometimes known as original cricket, although it is also colloquially referred to as bittle-battle.

Traditionally a game for women – but from very recently played by men too – its popularity has ebbed and flowed with the ages. It has never had a better following than today, and in addition to numerous ladies' stoolball clubs the game's

modern profile includes several mixed teams. No clubs or teams yet exist that are exclusively for men.

In recent years the clubs have been formed into divisions and leagues under an administrative body rather grandly titled The National Association of Stoolball. Despite the countrywide connotations of that name, and the staging each year of the National Stoolball Tournament, the game has only ever been played in Sussex and –

since the last century – on the fringes of Kent and Surrey.

The stoolball wicket is a foot-square piece of wood, 4in thick, mounted on a stake so that the top is 4ft 8in from the ground. Two wickets are used, spaced 16yds apart and guarded by two bats-women – or strikers – and overseen by two umpires. The square wicket was not, it appears, a form that was followed slavishly. A photograph taken near Bolney in 1891 shows a family game where the wicket is round.

Bowling is underarm only, using a hard, leather-covered ball smaller than those used by tennis players, and the wooden striking tools resemble long-handled table tennis bats. As for dress, the English tradition of 'sporting whites' holds sway: ladies wear white blouses and short white skirts; men take the field in white shorts and shirts.

Arlington

Map Ref: 87TQ5407

The date of the chapel in little Arlington church, whose shingled spire can be seen long before the village, is between 1066 and 1190 – but there is evidence to show that the site was occupied by an even earlier place of worship. Pilgrims on their way from the West Country to Canterbury would have rested at the great priory of St Pancras in Lewes, and made Arlington their next stop. Early written records of 1455 show that its 30 cows were let out to farmers, who paid for them in the beeswax used to light the shrines.

Inside are traces of soft pink and brown medieval wall paintings, and an unusual collection of items: Saxon pottery; part of an Ice Age bison horn; food-storage jars discovered in pieces under the church floor; a dark wooden chest with boards roughcut from a tree; and 18th-century horseshoes, discovered during the excavation of Arlington's 150-acre reservoir, which was completed in 1971. Now a nature reserve rich in wildfowl, the reservoir shore is the route of a circular walk. Vehicles can be left ½ mile from Berwick Railway station on the B2108, but the car park is set back from the road and not well signposted.

One mile east of Arlington village is Abbots Wood, which in the time of Henry I was owned by Battle

Arundel Castle's opulent great drawing room, recorded by an engraver when Queen Victoria visited in 1847

Abbey. Today it is owned by the Forestry Commission, which has designed a 1½-mile circular walk there and created a special 400yd trail for disabled people in wheelchairs.

Arundel

Map Ref: 85TQ0107

The prospect of Arundel seen from above the plain of the River Arun is spectacular. On the far side of the river houses climb up a steep hill, tier upon tier, towards on one side a fairytale castle, on the other a 19th-century Gothic cathedral beneath a lofty spire.

Built in the 11th century by Roger de Montgomery, the 1st Earl

Although it resembles a medieval stronghold, Arundel Castle is largely a Victorian sham

of Arundel, the castle has for over 700 years been the home of the Dukes of Norfolk and their forbears. It has been destroyed and rebuilt three times in its long history, and its present appearance owes much to the romanticism of 19th-century restorers. During the Civil War the Fitzalan Chapel – where many of the Dukes are buried – was badly damaged, and when rebuilt it was joined on to the 14th-century Parish Church of St Nicholas. To this day the church is divided, with half being Catholic (for the Duke's family) and half Anglican. Within the castle is a fine collection of furniture, tapestries, clocks and family portraits.

Arundel High Street winds up to the castle from the river bridge and is lined with a good mixture of shops, hostelries and restaurants – many hiding Tudor origins behind their 18th-century façades. Here can be found the town museum, and a fascinating little Toy and Military Museum. In the castle park international cricket teams play the Duchess of Norfolk's XI, and there are walks and boating at Swanbourne Lake. The famous Arun Bath Tub Race is held in August.

Some sources claim that the name Arundel came from *hirondelle*, French for the swallow or martin which appears on the coat of arms of the Earls of Arundel and is incorporated for the county. The bird is also now known as the Sussex martlet.

Another, more immediate avian connection is the Arundel Wildfowl Trust, one of the seven reserves founded by Sir Peter Scott. Situated in 60 acres of wetlands by the River Arun, it has a permanent collection of over 1,000 wildfowl, including species brought from all over the world as well as native birds. Habitats including ponds and reed beds are criss-crossed by public paths and overlooked by hides.

In school holidays the Trust runs special craft events for children, including weekday-afternoon sessions making masks, badges and brass rubbings of endangered species. Also popular are giant jigsaws in the reception area.

AA recommends:
Hotels: Norfolk Arms, High St, 3-star, *tel.* (0903) 882101

Howards, Crossbush, 2-star, *tel.* (0903) 882655

Burpham Country, Old Down, Burpham, 1-star, country-house, *tel.* (0903) 882160, (3m NE off A27)

Guesthouses: Arden, 4 Queens La, *tel.* (0903) 882544

Bridge House, 18 Queen St, *tel.* (0903) 882142

Swan Hotel, High St (inn), *tel.* (0903) 882314

Campsite: Maynards Caravan Park, Crossburgh, 2-pennants, *tel.* (0903) 882075, (1½m E on A27)

Barcombe

Map Ref: 87TQ4114

The Romans knew this village, and *Domesday* records that it had a church and three and a half mills – the half being explained by the fact that one of them spanned the river, so was partly in neighbouring Isfield. Modern Barcombe has several centres: Barcombe Cross, with its tile-hung houses and shops, a pub and the 16th-century Old Forge House; Barcombe Mills, a popular place for fishing and picnics; and a mile to the south, the flint-built parish church of St Mary – heart of the village until in the 17th century the plague decimated the population. Those who survived moved a mile away to build new homes at Barcombe Cross.

It has a tranquil setting, with flat farmland on one side and on the other a village duck pond, the 14th-century Court House, a large tiled barn and a thatched round shelter. The oldest part of the church is the 11th-century north wall, but other features include a 12th-century chancel, a 13th-century tower and a 14th-century font. Much was altered in 1879, with the Victorians' zeal for 'restoring' ecclesiastical buildings. The present pine roof replaced one made of chestnut, also called Poor Man's Oak; in medieval times people were forbidden to use oak or yew, the former being needed for building ships and the latter for making bows. Parsons were always required to grow yew in their churchyards, so there would always be plenty for the bowmen of England.

One other part of Barcombe well worth visiting is the riverside Anchor Inn, said to be the smallest pub in the south and built in 1790 for bargees. It is possible, from here, to take a boat three miles upstream. The pub stands at the end of a very narrow, twisting, 2-mile lane off the

The River Arun is a favourite refuge both for wintering wildfowl and native species that stay there all year round

road from Barcombe to Piltdown and Newick. The strangely-named Sungei Bar is explained by the fact that the owners lived in Malaysia, and *Sungei* is the Malay name for river.

Beachy Head

Map Ref: 87TV5895

The Normans had the right idea when they called this magnificent chalk cliff 'Beau Chef' – beautiful head. Just west of Eastbourne, it rises a dramatic 534ft above the sea and is the highest point on the south coast. To the west, between it and the Cuckmere Valley, are the majestic Seven Sisters hills – Haven Brow, Short Brow, Rough Brow, Brass Point, Flagstaff Point, Bailey's Hill and Went Hill – forming a square mile of nature reserve in which flowers and butterflies thrive amongst the springy downland turf. Dipping steeply to valleys in which there once ran ancient rivers, these hills are a delight for walkers and a challenge to marathon runners. There are two lighthouses – disused Belle Tout of 1831 at the top, and another in the sea below the vertical white cliffs.

Beachy Head Path, dedicated to the United Nations International Year of Peace of 1986, offers a 20-minute walk affording marvellous views over the coastline and Eastbourne seafront.

Information about the area can be found at the Signalman's Cottage, formally the Beachy Head Natural History Centre, which was built in 1898 for the Lloyd's signalman who relayed messages between London and ships around Beachy Head.

Beachy Head, where the Downs meet the sea, is the eastern end of the South Downs Way long-distance footpath

Berwick

Map Ref: 87TQ5105

Today all is peaceful in Berwick's little 12th-century church of St Michael and All Angels, which is surrounded by trees at the end of a lane on high ground close to the Downs. But in the 1940s it was the centre of fierce controversy when, with many church windows being shattered by World War II bombs, Bishop Bell of Chichester invited locally-resident Bloomsbury artists Duncan Grant and Vanessa Bell to paint murals on its whitewashed walls. Now, in the words of the originator of the scheme, Charles Reilly, the murals give an atmosphere that is 'like stepping out of a foggy England into Italy . . . a very real addition to the real wealth of the country'.

When Edward III issued a proclamation in the 14th century for every man to practise archery on the Sabbath, the men of Berwick sharpened their arrows on the tower by the 900-year-old font.

The 'Venus and Gladiator' floor mosaic at Bignor is one of the country's finest

Bignor

Map Ref: 85SU9814

In 1811 a ploughman working on the West Burton side of Bignor discovered a Roman site of such importance that the village was immediately assured wide and enduring fame. One of the largest in Britain, the find covered some 4½ acres and comprised a residence incorporating some 70 buildings around a courtyard within a walled enclosure. Probably the focus of a large and prosperous estate, the complex is thought to have replaced early wooden buildings in the 2nd century AD, and been occupied until the end of the 4th century.

Comprehensive excavations were later refilled to protect the remains from erosion – all except for a few rooms that were incorporated within protective huts. These feature parts of the original walls, mosaic floors, examples of Roman central heating and various *in situ* relics. One serves as a display area for coins, domestic items and other material retrieved from the site.

Usually overshadowed by its celebrated predecessor, Bignor itself is a pretty downland village that is interesting in its own right. Its mainly 13th-century church preserves a Norman chancel arch, and near by is a superb Sussex yeoman's cottage, complete with half-timbering and an overhanging first storey. High on the chalk ridge south of Bignor the South Downs Way crosses the ancient route of Roman Stane Street.

Bognor Regis

Map Ref: 85SZ9399

Wealthy and retired London hatter Sir Richard Hotham founded Bognor in 1787, when he built an hotel, assembly rooms and Hotham House and Park between the sea and the village of Bersted. He named it Hothampton, but it was not a success as a bathing resort. A little later the name Hothampton disappeared, and a new community grew up a mile away on the coast next to a fishing and smuggling hamlet. There are still lobster pots, nets and fishermen selling their catch on the beach at the older end of Bognor, while 18th-century buildings survive at the other, along with Hotham House. Hotham Park now accommodates Rainbow's End, a children's paradise featuring a huge adventure playground, resident clown and various animals.

In the 1800s Bognor was a select bathing-place for the carriage trade, where George III's daughter, Princess Charlotte, stayed for several summer seasons; Queen Victoria referred to it as 'dear little Bognor'. Later the resort declined – though it enjoyed a minor revival after the advent of the railway – but it was not until 1929 that it assumed full popularity once more. In that year King George V spent his convalescence at Bognor after a serious illness, and added Regis to the town's name to commemorate his stay.

All the usual sports facilities can be found in the resort, and there is a leisure centre near by. Butlin's Holiday Camp, renamed South Coast World, has been given a £40 million facelift, and is now open to day visitors. The multi-purpose Regis Centre offers various entertainments through the year, and a modern shopping centre

Ironwork like this Regency example at Bognor Regis was often made by local craftsmen pursuing a Sussex tradition

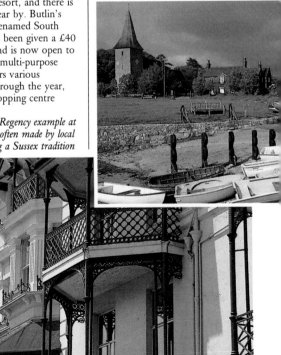

contrasts with the town's covered Victorian arcade and gardens.

Bognor Regis has a unique annual event – the International Clown's Convention – which was established in 1985.

Bosham

Map Ref: 84SU8004

Of the 13 villages encircling Chichester Harbour, Bosham – pronounced Bozzum – is the most famous, both for its history and its charm. It claims to be the place where Canute ordered the waves to go back, and modern motorists doubtless wish they could do the same when they park too near the high-tide mark.

Although the Irish monk Dicul built a tiny monastery at Bosham, it is Bishop Wilfrid who is credited with bringing Christianity to this pagan outpost in AD681 – and with teaching the starving South Saxons how to fish. There is a legend that marauding Danes landed and carried away one of the bells of Holy Trinity, but when the Saxons rang the remaining ones the stolen

Tradition has it that a daughter of King Canute is buried in Bosham's lovely Saxon and Norman church

bell sank, wrecking the Norsemen's ship. Ever since, when the church bells are rung, it is said that the bell under the sea chimes in reply.

It seems certain that Harold set sail in 1064 from Bosham to encounter William of Normandy before the Battle of Hastings. The Bayeux Tapestry depicts Harold outside Bosham church, and the name of Bosham appears on it – spelt the same as today.

Bosham was an important port in the Middle Ages, and boasted several mills that ground corn from the grain ships. A water-mill on the quay now houses the local Sailing Club. From the late 1800s into the 20th century, oyster smacks worked from Bosham, many built in a local shipyard which survived until the last war, when sections of the Mulberry Harbour were built there.

AA recommends:
Hotel: Millstream, Bosham La, 2-star, *tel.* (0243) 573234
Guesthouse: White Barn, Crede La, *tel.* (0243) 573113

Bramber

Map Ref: 86TQ1910

Now little more than a main street, this village was once a busy port on the River Adur estuary and in early times was known as *Portus Adurni*. William de Braose, friend of the Conqueror, built the castle – of which only a few remains have survived – on a small hill above the village (see page 52), and the priory of Sele downstream at Upper Beeding. After the estuary silted up Bramber declined into a small village. Charles II, on his flight to the coast after the Battle of Worcester in 1651, had a narrow escape at Bramber from an encounter with Parliamentary troops, and took refuge in the house of St Mary. Described as 'the best example of late 15th-century timber-framing in Sussex', this monastic inn changed hands in 1985 and was lovingly restored by its new owner. The beautiful interior contains fine panelled rooms with furniture, pictures and *objets d'art*.

Bramber is also the home of a most unusual museum – the House of Pipes – in which one man has amassed a huge collection of smoking paraphernalia numbering some 35,000 items from 150 countries, and spanning 1,500 years. The museum has received a British Tourist Authority commendation.

The finest and largest late Bronze Age spearhead hoard recovered in England this century was found in a field just outside Bramber in 1981, and can be seen at Worthing Museum.

AA recommends:
Guesthouse: Castle Hotel, The Street (inn), *tel.* (0903) 812102

Regency Resorts

When the Prince Regent came to Brighton for the first time in 1783 he was just a few weeks past his 21st birthday, and by the time of his last visit, some 47 years later, the town had been transformed. The words 'Regency' and 'Brighton' are almost synonymous, although other towns along the Sussex coast were similarly influenced by a style of architecture which was actually in vogue much longer than the Regency of the Prince of Wales.

Regency architecture grew out of neo-classical Georgian – almost literally, in the case of the Brighton Pavilion. Its prominent pseudo-eastern spires and domes were commissioned by the Prince Regent from the architect Nash to replace Henry Holland's earlier work. The Pavilion was by no means universally admired when first completed – indeed, it was generally considered to be the height of bad taste. It was, none-the-less, fun – a far cry from the 20th century box-building which has sadly affected much of the town.

Colourful and flippant, the Royal Pavilion contrasts with the restrained and elegant seafront architecture of Brighton and Hove – the Royal Crescent; the fashionable Steine; terraces, squares and crescents; and the quaintly charming Lanes or 'twittens' in the centre of town. Here, antique collectors and tourists rub shoulders daily both in and outside the summer season, probably not realising that most of the houses in this originally medieval quarter were built in the 18th and 19th centuries by architects returning to earlier styles.

Lewes and Chichester both pre-

Eastbourne pier retains the grace seen by these children in 1910

serve examples of Regency architecture. Opposite Anne of Cleves' House in Lewes is a small terrace of late-Georgian houses, and three parallel streets leading out of the High Street have good Regency buildings. Chichester's streets – particularly those in the quarter known as the Pallant – contain many listed houses, the majority of which were built during the Georgian and Regency period. Nash himself built the New Market House in 1807.

A medley of meerschaums and clays, part of the House of Pipes display at Bramber

A popular form of candied sugar

George IV's Royal Pavilion in Brighton was designed by John Nash around a classical house by Henry Holland

Brighton

Map Ref: 86TQ3105

An all-the-year-round holiday resort with something for everyone to enjoy, this town of contrasts has elegant Regency squares; the narrow and traffic-free Lanes, with their antique shops, jewellers, pubs and cafés; smart shops; and cheap, lively markets. Above all, it has the magical, Chinese-style Royal Pavilion – built in 1822 for the Prince Regent, later to become George IV. Today it is fully furnished in the splendour of its original style, including many items on loan from the Queen.

Not only is there plenty to see in Brighton, but plenty to do as well. Fine days are made for riding the Volks seafront railway to Brighton Marina – Europe's largest – which was designed for over 2,000 yachts and has a locked inner harbour. Historic boats can be seen there, and there is a restaurant close at hand. Palace Pier offers a ¼-mile stroll out to sea; the Dolphinarium is ever popular; and a day at the races never loses its appeal. At the

William IV made his mark in Brighton too – on cast-iron lamp-posts

King Alfred Leisure Centre in Hove are pools, a solarium, sauna and ten-pin bowling.

When the sun is not shining, there is the excellent Brighton Art Gallery and Museum to enjoy. Its Fashion Gallery has displays of clothing from 1830 to the present day, and there is a superb collection of furniture and furnishings from the Art Deco and Art Nouveau eras –plus a display of Brighton's early history. Preston Manor features original 17th-, 18th- and 19th-century English furnishings, and the Booth Museum has fascinating displays about natural history.

The Theatre Royal has a Victorian interior and stages many London productions, while the Brighton Centre features concerts, dances and sporting championships. The Dome presents concerts all year round, as well as a Summer Season.

In Hove – west of Brighton but joined to it – is The British Engineerium, which will entrance even the most non-technically minded. A unique museum of applied sciences and technology, it has a fascinating display of models and full-size engines – some of which are 'steamed' every Sunday and on public holidays.

AA recommends:

Hotels: Courtlands, 22 The Drive, Hove, 3-star, *tel.* (0273) 731055
Sackville, 189 Kingsway, Hove, 3-star, *tel.* (0273) 736292
Granville, 125 King's Rd, 2-star, *tel.* (0273) 26302
Whitehaven, 34 Wilbury Rd, Hove, 2-star,

tel. (0273) 778355
Restaurants: Eaton, Eaton Gdns, Hove, 3-fork, *tel.* (0273) 738921
La Marinade, 77 St George's Rd, Kemptown, 2-fork, *tel.* (0273) 600992
Stubbs of Ship Street, 14 Ship St, 2-fork, *tel.* (0273) 204005
French Connection, 11 Little East St, 1-fork, *tel.* (0273) 24454
Guesthouses: Adelaide Hotel, 51 Regency Sq, *tel.* (0273) 205286
Cavalaire House, 34 Upper Rock Gdns, Kemptown, *tel.* (0273) 696899
Prince Regent Hotel, 29 Regency Sq, *tel.* (0273) 29962
Twenty One, 21 Charlotte St, Marine Pde, *tel.* (0273) 686450
Self Catering: 12B Brunswick Rd, Hove (flat), *tel.* (0273) 507381
54 Cornwall Gdns (house), *tel.* (07917) 2219
Garages: Endeavour Mtr Co, 90 Preston Rd, *tel.* (0273) 550211
Evans Halshaw, 9-17 Old Shoreham Rd, Portslade-by-Sea, *tel.* (0273) 422552
Lee Mtrs, Church Pl, Kemptown, *tel.* (0273) 684022
Wadham Stringer, 154 Old Shoreham Rd, Hove, *tel.* (0273) 26264

The quaint alleys and shops of The Lanes occupy the site of old Brighton

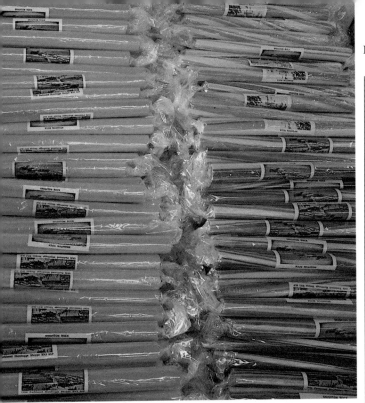

Bury

Map Ref: 85TQ0113

Bury is a pretty, leafy little place, lying off the beaten track. Its houses are of Wealden style, many of them being built of sandstone, few of flint, although the downland and its chalk is near by.

The village runs down to the River Arun opposite Amberley, and until 1957 there was a ferry service, with a ferrywoman whose place was later taken by her daughter. Women seem to have played a prominent part in village life. In 1796, the single ladies of Bury were beaten in a cricket match by the married ladies' team. They then jointly challenged any other ladies' team in the county. Then there were the two women by the names of Big Ben and Mendoza who were opponents in a prize fight before a large crowd. Big Ben won. There was also said to be a village female witch (witches can be male or female in Sussex), who described future spouses to young men and girls.

In Bury House, a 20th-century Tudor mansion, John Galsworthy lived the last seven years of his life; and his ashes were scattered on the historic slopes of Bury Hill.

AA recommends:
Garage: Turners, Bury Common, *tel.* (079881) 417

Butser Hill

Map Ref: 84SU7120

After their stately progress through much of East and the whole of West Sussex, the South Downs cross into Hampshire and immediately culminate in the huge chalk bastion of 889ft Butser Hill – the highest in the range. Dotted with prehistoric round barrows, this colossus is the start of an ancient ridgeway that once penetrated to the heart of Wessex. Some of that way, to the reserve and hillfort on Old Winchester Hill, is open

Butser, focal point of the 1,400-acre Queen Elizabeth Country Park, is one of the few Hampshire Downs where sheep-cropped turf can be felt underfoot. The animals are there at the instigation of the county council, and are gradually turning the clock back to past days of wool and wild chalkland flowers.

A special feature of the Country Park is its Ancient Farm Research Project, in which old ways of life are reconstructed and archaeological theories tested. Of particular note is the demonstration Iron Age farm, complete with thatched huts, wattle fences and everything from crops to utensils as close to the supposed originals as possible.

The Country Park itself has modern beechwoods and yew-filled combes as well as downland, and includes nature reserves managed by the Hampshire and Isle of Wight Naturalists' Trust. Such a great diversity of habitats encourages a rich and varied flora and fauna, some of which can be observed from waymarked trails. Demonstrations of ancient crafts and farming practices are given regularly. Refreshments are available too, and there is a picnic site.

Chanctonbury

Map Ref: 85TQ1312

Chanctonbury Ring, distinctive with its rounded cap of beech trees, has all the mystery and other-worldliness appropriate to its vast age and is at the centre of numerous local legends. One in particular tells of dark riders who travelled between Chanctonbury and Cissbury – black-clothed, riding black horses and followed by black hounds. They were Odin and his followers, collectors of souls, and it is not long since people would swear to have heard the thunder of their hooves on moonless nights.

Many finds on Chanctonbury testify to early cultures, and it may in Neolithic times have been a sacred meeting place. Local people claim to have experienced curious events or sensations when up at the Ring, such as horses shying away from unseen hazards, dogs refusing to enter the grove, the lack of birdsong and strong rumours of witches' covens. On a more light-hearted note, Morris men dance at Chanctonbury Ring late at night on May Day Eve, though who of their audience remembers that Hallowe'en, May Day Eve and the Midsummer Solstice were all regarded as sacred by past cultures?

The trees that today shield the Ring from wind and weather were planted in 1760 by Charles Goring of Wiston House, which stands at the foot of the downland. A lord of the manor, Goring realised a childhood dream by so covering the summit – and even today people say Mother Goring has her cap on when mist shrouds Chanctonbury.

Chanctonbury Ring's distinctive beech clump grows on earthworks that were part of an elaborate defence system

Charlton, *see* Singleton

Chichester

Map Ref: 84SU8604

The Romans named Chichester *Regnum* and built the walls, remnants of which encompass substantial traces of the original city plan. Four main streets from the points of the compass intersected where the 16th-century Market Cross – or Butter Cross – now stands. This was donated by Bishop Storey to help poor traders. After the Romans came Cissa the Saxon, who is said to have changed the name to Cissa's Ceastre.

One of the earliest buildings is St Mary's Hospital, which was founded in the late 12th century. Its almshouses, built into the hospital

John Piper's altar-screen tapestry brings a flare of colour to the sober stone interior of Chichester Cathedral

wards, are still lived in. In the medieval Guildhall the great artist and poet William Blake was tried for high treason in 1804, and acquitted. Chichester today is a mainly Georgian city, known for its 18th-century streets of houses. One of the best is Pallant House, which was built about 1712 and is also called Dodo House, from the curious stone birds on its gateposts. In Eastgate Square is an 18th-century house where Keats wrote part of *The Eve of St Agnes*. Chichester's famous Festival Theatre, built in 1962, is not its first – a predecessor stood for many years in South Street.

Above all Chichester is a cathedral city, as proclaimed by the spire that can be seen for miles on the coastal plain and from out at sea. Founded at Selsey, the cathedral was moved in the 11th century to Chichester and stood on the site of the Roman forum. The present building is mainly Norman, with later additions, and contains various works by 20th-century artists. Included are paintings by Graham Sutherland and Hans Feibusch, a tapestry by John Piper, monuments by John Flaxman, a stained-glass window by Marc Chagall and a font by John Skelton.

A real must for the visitor is the Mechanical Music and Doll's Museum, a superb collection that was brought together by one family and is now housed in a redundant church. All the machines have been restored and are demonstrated for visitors, including a fascinating mechanical and clockwork Belgian piano with a whole gamut of musical instruments built into it, sounding like a full dance band. Most of the exhibits span a period from 1830 to 1930, with the notable exception of a magnificent fair organ made locally in 1980.

In keeping with the period is the Doll Collection, containing many German and French bisque-headed dolls, and other curiosities appropriate to the era grace the walls. In a converted side chapel is a Victorian parlour, complete with maid and mistress, birds under glass domes and a working magic lantern.

Near Chichester is the Tangmere Airfield, a famous fighter aerodrome from 1917 to 1970 and now the home of a museum which tells the story of military flying. Special emphasis is placed on the air war over the south of England in general, and Sussex in particular, from 1939 to 1945. Poignant memorabilia is displayed in the Battle of Britain Hall, and a special exhibit deals with the Lysanders which flew out secretly at night to make contact with Resistance movements and secret agents.

AA recommends:
Hotels: Chichester Lodge, Westhampnett, 3-star, *tel.* (0243) 786351 Dolphin & Anchor, West St, 3-star, *tel.* (0243) 785121
Restaurant: Aspen Tree, 149 St Pancras, 2-fork, *tel.* (0243) 788724
Guesthouse: Bedford Hotel, Southgate, *tel.* (0243) 785766
Self Catering: Hunston Mill, Selsey Rd, Hunston, *tel.* (0243) 783375, (2½m S of B2145)
Campsite: Southern Leisure Centre, Vinnetrow Rd, 3-pennants, *tel.* (0243) 787715
Garages: Automac Ltd, 1-3 Bognor Rd, *tel.* (0243) 782451
D Rowe & Co, The Hornet, *tel.* (0243) 788100
Wadham Stringer, Terminus Rd, *tel.* (0243) 781331

Chichester's graceful cathedral spire, by Gilbert Scott in the 19th century, replaces one by Sir Christopher Wren

A mile or so north east of Chiddingly is Stonehill House, a superb example of 15th-century timber framing

Now there is a Jack and Jill Preservation Society and Jill is normally open on Sundays.

Clayton also has a slightly bizarre tunnel entrance built, in 1840, at the cost of £90,000 for the London, Brighton and South Coast Railway. It consists of two turreted towers in yellow brick, with arrow slits and castellations, standing on either side of a pointed arch which spans the line near the roadside.

Cocking

Map Ref: 84SU8717

The bright, buttercup-yellow paint which adorns the eaves and window frames of cottages in and around Cocking is there to identify them as belonging to the Cowdray estate. Features of the restored Norman church, which is mainly 14th century, are a Norman tub font and a 13th-century wall painting.

West of the village are two lofty hills well known to walkers of the South Downs Way – Cocking Down and Linch Down. The former offers wide views to Chichester Harbour and the cathedral spire; the latter rises to 818ft and is the third highest in the South Downs range.

East of Cocking, at Heyshott, is a charming little flint church which dates mainly from the 13th century. Nearby Dunford House was the birthplace in 1804 of Richard Cobden, an outspoken and influential exponent of free trade.

Chiddingly

Map Ref: 87TQ5414

Tradition has it that the Jefferay family, one-time local lords of the manor, once laid a line of cheeses from their home at Chiddingly Place to the church door to prevent their feet getting dirty. Judging by their impressive monument in the church the story could be true, because two of the figures are standing on large round pieces of Sussex marble – possibly cheeses! The church itself has a rare 15th-century stone spire, which stands about 128ft high and can be seen for miles around. Just along the road is the Wealden Way path. Chiddingly Festival, held each year in October, is an event of music, art exhibitions, theatre and films.

Cissbury Ring

Map Ref: 85TQ1307

Situated 603ft high on the Downs behind Worthing, Cissbury Ring (NT) covers 60 acres and is named after the Saxon chief, Cissa. However, it is much older, dating from at least 3000BC – when Neolithic man settled in the chalk areas of Sussex and worked the hills for flint. Mines were sunk to the best seams, and at Cissbury is a complex of shafts and galleries that are probably the earliest examples of industrial activity in Britain. Hollows and mounds are the present-day evidence of their existence.

Some 200 shafts have been identified, and finds have included flint tools, antler picks, shovels made from the shoulder blades of oxen, pig and red deer – and even a miner's lamp. Worthing Museum has a splendid Cissbury collection.

Most of the visible remains – which gives this landmark its distinctive shape – survive from a long, oval Iron Age hillfort with a great rampart and external ditch-and-bank defences. Romano-British

farmers ploughed the interior of the fort, and in around AD300 it was refortified against the Saxons.

Clayton

Map Ref: 86TQ3014

It might be a tiny hamlet – tucked away at the foot of the Downs near Brighton – but many have passed this way since the Romans built a road from Croydon to Portslade right through it. The sturdy little church was built in the 11th century and the marvellous frescoes on its walls are thought to have been painted at the same time. They show the Last Judgment and Christ in Glory and were only discovered after church restoration in the 1890s.

Standing like two sentinels on the hill above are the Jack and Jill windmills. Jill is a white post-mill built originally in Brighton about 1821 and brought here, across the Downs, by teams of oxen in 1852. Jack, a brick tower-mill, was built on the site in 1896 and the two worked together until about 1907.

Jill Mill at Clayton has been fully restored and pays its own way in bags of stone-ground wholemeal flour

Coolham

Map Ref: 86TQ1222

Down a narrow lane off the Billingshurst–Coolham road is an ancient half-timbered farmhouse with the strange name of the 'Blue Idol', overlooking a peaceful garden of lawns and apple trees. In 1691 William Penn founded the Meeting House of the Friends of Thakeham in one half of the house, and worshipped there regularly. He lived four miles away at Warminghurst, and would ride over on horseback – his wife and children travelling in an oxen-drawn family coach.

During the 17th century the Friends were severely persecuted, and a burial ground near by is said to hold the remains of many local Quakers who perished in Horsham Gaol. In 1674 Penn used his high-born personal influence to acquire from the Crown a refuge in America, with religious freedom for the Friends.

The Meeting House closed from 1793 to 1869, when it reopened – and it has remained open ever since.

Cowdray Park, *see* Midhurst

Cuckfield

Map Ref: 86TQ3024

George IV used to stop here on his
way from London to Brighton and
change horses at the King's Head,
then on the other side of the road.
However, Cuckfield's (pronounced
Cookfield) history goes back to
Norman times when it had a
hunting lodge and chapel. It became
an important centre when Sussex
was producing the country's iron
nails, cannons and horseshoes. In
the Civil War Cromwell's soldiers
stabled their horses in the church
and, so the story goes, the crack in
the font was caused by a kick from
one of them!

In the 1780s a stage coach, the
Brightelmstone and Cuckfield
Machine, used to pass through here
three days a week but by the end of
the 18th century over 50 coaches a
day travelled through the town. An
American kept up a coach service
here until World War I – when the
horses were taken by the army.

Today many of the old houses
still line the busy High Street. At
the top is an interesting little
museum over the local library,
showing items connected with
Cuckfield's past. The church, at the
other end of the street, was built
around the 14th century although
the roof is 15th century, with
decorations added in 1886. Outside,
the front doors of three cottages
open directly on to the churchyard.

The residents of Cuckfield are
very proud. In 1965, after a
disagreement with the local council,
they declared themselves to be 'The
Independent State of Cuckfield'.
Now a mayor is elected annually
and everyone may vote as many
times as they like – as long as they
pay a penny each time. This is not
quite as corrupt as it sounds
because all the proceeds go to
charity! After the election, the new
mayor rides through the town in a
donkey-drawn carriage leading a
carnival procession.

AA recommends:
Hotels: Ockenden Manor, Ockenden La,
3-star, *tel.* (0444) 416111
Hilton Park, 2-star, *tel.* (0444) 454555

Devil's Dyke

Map Ref: 86TQ2511

Views from the top of the Dyke –
693ft above the sea and four miles
west of Brighton – extend right
across the Weald; with binoculars,
it is said that glimpses of Windsor
Castle can be caught through a gap
in the North Downs!

In prehistoric times a hilltop fort
stood here, and early Iron Age oxen
bones and fragments of pottery
have been found in the area. At the
turn of the century cable cars swung

*Ascribed to Flynton, 16th-century
Cuckfield Place was styled 'Rookwood'
in H Ainsworth's story of that name*

*View from the South Downs Way of
the Devil's Dyke – one of Sussex's
most famous beauty spots – and the
charming village of Poynings*

across the Dyke; there was a
funicular railway to the village of
Poynings below and, until the
1930s, a railway connected it with
Brighton.

Today it is popular with walkers,
model aircraft enthusiasts, kite flyers
and hang-glider pilots. The view
from the first-floor restaurant of the
Inn at the Dyke is stunning.

Ditchling

Map Ref: 86TQ3215

For the last 70 years or so
Ditchling, at the foot of the Downs,
has been famous for the artists and
craftsmen who have lived there,
including Eric Gill, Tadlek Beutlich,
Ethel Mairet and Frank Brangwyn.
Others flourish there today. The
village is ancient, with earliest
records going back to 765 – after
which the manor passed to Alfred
the Great, Edward the Confessor
and William de Warenne. The
oldest building today is the flint-
and-stone 13th-century church,
which is built on the site of an even
earlier one. The stone is from
Normandy. Close by are a village
green which was a farmyard until
1965, a village pond and an ancient
burial mound. The 16th-century
Wing's Place, brick and timber-
framed with endearingly sloping
roofs, is known as Anne of Cleves'

Devil and Dragon

The most famous place associated with the Devil on the South Downs is his Dyke – a deep cleft in the chalk near Poynings, inaccessible to the motorist and a haven for chalk-loving wild flowers and plants.

Tradition has it that the Devil planned to destroy the Wealden churches by digging a trench from the Downs to the sea and flooding them. An old woman who observed him working on his trench lit a candle and held it to her window, the better to see him, and the light caused the cocks to crow. Thinking that the sun was rising, the Devil departed in high haste without completing his task.

In high summer during the 19th century it was not unusual for the Devil's Dyke to be the destination for up to 100 carriages each day, all bringing sightseers to the viewpoint and the cleft. Later, a cable railway was briefly established across the Dyke, with a funicular lift to carry the visiting crowds up the steep side of the cleft.

On Bow Hill, a spur of the South Downs overlooking Chichester, are the Devil's Humps, a line of Bronze Age bell and bowl barrows sited

above Kingley Vale and its famous grove of ancient yews. As the yew has long been associated with the Christian church, perhaps they were planted to counteract the brooding influence of the Devil on the heights above.

Satan was certainly busy in this part of the prehistoric world, as further north between Chilgrove and Elsted on Treyford Hill are five bell-shaped barrows called the Devil's Jumps.

Old representation of Belial – another name for the Devil – confronting his demons and victims at the gate of hell

At Lyminster a dragon once dwelt in the Knucker Hole – one of a series of pools alongside the public footpath to Arundel. The beast was despatched by a local lad whose tombstone, by the font in Lyminster church, is said to represent the sword with which he despatched the unfortunate beast.

house – though there is no proof that she ever lived here.

It is also a lively village, with food shops among the tea shops, four pubs, a picture-framer, an art gallery and a craft centre. The Victorian village school houses a Museum of Local Life, the building having been saved from demolition by sisters Hilary and Joanna Bourne, who bought it to create the museum. Special exhibitions are also held.

Near by is Ditchling Common, a

188-acre Country Park with a short circular nature trail marked by wooden posts to and from the car park. Also close by is the magnificent 813ft Ditchling Beacon, where fires were lit to warn of the Armada four centuries ago. On a clear day the Beacon affords beautiful views over to the sea and across the Weald. It was given to the National Trust by Sir Stephen Demetriadi in memory of his son Richard, who was killed in the

Battle of Britain, 1940. A board shows three circular walks of varying length that can be followed from the top, and on the way down along Beacon Road the walker can stop at the local vineyard to sample the wine – and maybe invest in a Morning After Hangover Herb Draught, or wine mustards.

AA recommends:
Guesthouse: Bull Hotel, 2 High St (inn), *tel.* (07918) 3147

A popular aspect of Eastbourne's cultural life is music on the Esplanade – a 2½-mile seaside walk among terraces and gardens

Dawn walkers on Eastbourne sands at low tide are likely to meet long-liners unhooking the night's catch

Eastbourne

Map Ref: 87TV6098

Just over 200 years ago in 1780 George III brought his children to Eastbourne (to a house on Marine Parade, near the pier), and gave the town the royal seal of approval. Today it is still the aristocrat of the south-coast holiday resorts, with its three-mile, three-tiered, flower-lined and immaculately kept promenade; 200 acres of parks and gardens; a splendidly preserved Victorian pier; a bandstand; and safe sands.

It has excellent shops, and interesting ones too. As well as the ubiquitous chain stores, near the railway station there is an Enterprise Centre with many tiny stall-like shops and a twice-weekly outdoor market; and The Labyrinth, with its craft shops, in Mark Lane.

In the Old Town is Pilgrims, a timbered house that goes back to the 12th century and has underground passages linking it to the 12th-century church of St Mary and the 13th-century Lamb Inn.

The town has museums and art galleries; summer shows, ballet and opera at the Congress Theatre; West End productions at the Devonshire Park Theatre; and a marvellous variety of events throughout the year at the Winter Garden including wrestling, ballroom dancing, antique fairs, and flower and motor shows.

For children there is Treasure Island, Eastbourne's award-winning play centre with an acre of paddling pools, sand-pits, a Spanish galleon, lighthouse, model zebras, elephants, lions and crocodiles. Parents can relax there too, though they are only admitted with children.

For the energetic holidaymaker Eastbourne has golf courses, two sailing clubs, over 60 tennis courts, bowling, miniature golf, squash, badminton, table tennis, horse riding and fishing. The new Ball Park, with its sports and leisure club facilities, is the only one of its kind in the country. Eastbourne is also the beginning (or end!) of the South Downs Way (see page 16).

East Dean's 13th-century Tiger Inn

East Dean, East Sussex

Map Ref: 87TV5597

Off the A259 at the foot of the hill from Friston is a picture-book village green with a pub, flint cottages and a general store. The whitewashed Tiger Inn, built in 1298, called itself The Tiger for several hundred years before it was realised that the animal in the Bardolf family coat of arms, after which the pub was named, was in fact a leopard. Once a favourite haunt for smugglers who would bring their booty in from Birling Gap just a mile away, many of its dark beams are said to have been made out of old wrecks. Today it is popular with local people and visitors. The Hunt meets there, and

on bank holidays Morris Dancers perform outside.

In the 18th century, Parson Jonathan Darby is said to have made a cave in the cliffs at Birling Gap, though there are two versions of why he did so: one was as a refuge from Mrs Darby; the other as a shelter for shipwrecked sailors! Known as Parson Darby's Hole, it disappeared through cliff erosion around 1851, when the Belle Tout lighthouse was built.

East Dean's 11th-century church (down Lower Road from The Green) has a Saxon tower, a tapsell gate pivoting on a central post, and five bells – two of which are pre-Reformation and bear Latin inscriptions. One of these, says the church guide, has rather 'a boastful ring about it'. Roughly translated it means 'No bell under the sky is better than I.'

The old laundry was once the home of the descendants of the Pendrill family, who hid Charles II in an oak tree. Wires of the first telegraph connecting Britain with the Continent were carried over the Downs from here to under-sea cables at Birling Gap.

AA recommends:
Self Catering: Birlingdean, 81 Michel Dene Rd, *tel.* (03215) 2303

East Dean, West Sussex
see Singleton

Edburton

Map Ref: 85TQ2311

The unclassified road which runs westwards from the A23 at Newtimber Place is one of the most beautiful of those which hug the northern foot of the Downs. It winds through Poynings and Fulking until it joins the A2037 Upper Beeding–Henfield road. At the tiny hamlet of Edburton the escarpment is at one of its highest points, and rises so steeply that the Downs look like mountains. On their top there is a mound and ditch known as Castle Rings, the remains

Salmon from Scottish rivers meet a delectable end at Edburton's smokeries

of an 11th-century fort.

The small, 13th-century flintstone church of St Andrew contains one of three rare, medieval lead fonts in Sussex and a 17th-century 'black-letter' Bible, printed in Old English heavy type. The Reverend George Keith is its most notable incumbent in having been a member of the Society for the Propagation of the Gospel's first missionary to America in 1702. In recognition, on its 250th anniversary, the SPG gave the church a window.

Edburton today is best known as the unlikely home of a salmon smokery. Geoffrey Harris farmed with his father at Perching Manor Farm near by. His father-in-law, a famous smoker in Norfolk, offered to teach him the tricks of the trade, and in 1964 Geoffrey Harris set up a smokery in some old farm buildings at Edburton. Springs Smoked Salmon has never looked back, and it is now the largest family-run smokery in the South East. The process of smoking is a well-kept secret. All Geoffrey Harris will say is that the fish is oak-smoked in the traditional way, and only wild Scotch salmon are used.

The Cuckmere Valley at Exceat has wild habitats including chalk slopes, a shingle shore, fresh and brackish water – and the river itself

Exceat

Map Ref: 87TV5199

The Cuckmere, as it ribbons its way into the sea, must be one of the most beautiful river estuaries in England. It is the only river in Sussex never to have had a port built at its mouth, but just inland is Exceat (pronounced Excete) – a Saxon fishing village until raids by the French and the Black Death drove the people away.

In 1974 East Sussex County Council opened an Interpretation Centre in a converted 18th-century barn by the river, and there is also the excellent Living World Museum of butterflies, bees, spiders, snails, ants and marine life there. Both are part of the Seven Sisters Country Park, which covers about 700 acres of the Cuckmere Valley and part of the Seven Sisters cliffs. It can be explored by circular trail, and – by prior arrangement – the Head Ranger will guide visitors over chalk grassland where 45 different wildflowers grow and where, by the river, can be seen swans, mallards, herons and geese.

The silver-washed fritillary might be seen in Friston Forest, above Exceat

Falmer

Map Ref: 86TQ3508

Situated between Lewes and Brighton, this village was cut in half in the 1970s, when the A27 was built right through it. Now a pedestrian bridge enables villagers on one side (with church and pond) to visit the shop and pub on the other, but many still have not forgiven the planners for dividing their community.

A 12th-century church here was pulled down in 1815, and the present one of flint and brick built to take its place. A handle-less pump stands by the pond and in the village hall, once the old school house, ladies of the village serve tea, coffee and home-made cakes on Sunday afternoons in aid of the upkeep of church and hall. On the other side of the footbridge is an unusual war memorial: a flower-filled horse trough. Near by is Sussex University in Stanmer Park, opened in 1962 as the first university to be built after World War II.

Findon

Map Ref: 85TQ1208

The Great Sussex Sheep Fair has been held at Findon every September since the 13th century, and each year the auctioneers report good business. As many as 20,000 sheep are brought to the fair, sometimes from long distances, and among the farmers mingle hordes of pleasure-seekers who flock there for the amusements and side shows. In the old days cattle and horses were also sold, and fortune-telling gypsies and a boxing booth were parts of an equally colourful scene.

It is just as well that nowadays sheep arrive by rail and road transporters, for there would be no grazing left if they were brought on the hoof, as used to be the case. Older people can still remember when thousands of animals were driven to the fair along the old droveways, some of which survive as roads across the Downs.

Findon village has succeeded in resisting the encroachment of nearby Worthing, and its white cottages and old inn nestle quietly under the Downs.

Long connected with horses, the village is home to the Josh Gifford racing stables – where 1981 Grand National winner Aldaniti was trained – and numbers the legendary Captain Ryan Price among its élite trainers. Captain Price, the Master of Findon, produced Classic Flat and National Hunt winners with equal facility for 30 years.

Firle

Map Ref: 87TQ4607

Five miles from Lewes, this once feudal village of flint cottages lies at the foot of the Downs and beneath Firle Beacon, which rises steeply to 718ft behind it. The blacksmith, miller, tailor, bootmaker, butcher, baker and harness maker who used to live there have all gone, but the village still has its ancient church, an old pub and Firle Place – home of the Gage family since the 15th century, and lived in today by the 7th Viscount. Set in parkland and open to the public in the summer, the original Tudor mansion, was built around 1487 and remodelled in the 18th century.

Inside is a magnificent collection of Sèvres porcelain and fine English and French furniture, while in the drawing rooms, Long Gallery and Great Hall are hung paintings by Van Dyck, Gainsborough, Reynolds and Fra Bartolomeo. Many are of family ancestors, and one of them – General Thomas Gage, the younger son of the 1st Viscount – became Commander in Chief of the British forces in America, and was serving at the outbreak of the American War of Independence. Another ancestor, a botanist, is said to have grown the first English greengage at Firle Place.

Near the back entrance to the park is the little church of St Peter, most of which dates from the 14th and 15th centuries. The tower, nave and chancel are early 13th century and the north door 12th century. The vestry has Gage monuments and was built between 1556 and 1559. A magnificent 20th-century contribution to the church is John Piper's *Tree of Life* window, which was installed in 1985 in memory of the 6th Viscount Gage.

From the top of Firle Beacon a breathtaking view can be enjoyed over to the sea and to the Cuckmere Valley.

Firle village from Firle Beacon, a lofty chalk hill where fires would once have been lit to warn of invasion

Memorabilia of some five centuries is preserved at Firle Place

forgotten until rediscovered by a trench digger in 1960. Subsequent excavations by the Sussex Archaeological Trust revealed a palace that could have come from Rome itself, and was possibly the home of King Cogidubnus, pro-Empire ruler of the Chichester-based Regenses tribe.

Much of the huge site lies beneath a main road and nearby houses, but a large part – including the whole of the north wing – has been roofed over and can be visited. Catwalks over the remains allow close study of major features such as mosaic floors, tesselated pavements and hypocaust heating systems, while smaller items found during excavation are displayed in a well-furbished museum. Part of the large garden around which the palace was built has been restored and planted with species that would have been grown there in Roman times.

Roman hypocaust – an underfloor heating system – excavated at Fishbourne

Fishbourne

Map Ref: 84SU8304

The largest and richest Roman palace found in Britain, Fishbourne exceeds even Bignor in archaeological importance and is remarkable in belonging to an early phase of the occupation.

Records of Roman remains having been found at Fishbourne go back to 1805, but the site was

Fittleworth

Map Ref: 85TQ0119

In H V Morton's *I Saw Two Englands*, Fittleworth is an acknowledged Sussex beauty spot 'that looks . . . as if it has grown up as naturally out of the soil as the oak trees and hedges'.

Though sadly cut in half by the main A283 road from Petersfield, Fittleworth retains much of the charm that has over the years attracted famous artists to the village. Many of them stayed at the old Swan Inn, which still displays evidence of their talents and features an unusual gallows sign. Other frequent visitors are traditionally anglers out to try their luck on local stretches of the River Rother, or farther downstream where it joins the Arun at Stopham. Picturesque old buildings in the village include a water-mill. The church, though of the Early English and Decorated periods, was restored in 1871.

Ancient Yews

Within the Kingley Vale National Nature Reserve, owned by the Nature Conservancy Council, is probably the finest yew forest extant in Europe. Nature reserves may be a modern phenomenon, but preservation of the yew is not, and it was protected until the reign of Elizabeth I for making longbows – England's superior weapon against the crossbow.

Probably because of its longevity (100 years is nothing in the life of a yew), from the days of antiquity the tree has been looked upon as a symbol of immortality. According to some sources, its presence in churchyards deterred witchcraft and grave robbers – but despite such legends depicting it as a force against evil, its dark and gloomy appearance suggests the very opposite.

Kingley Vale has long been known for its ancient yew groves, of which 20 500-year-old giants survive. However, younger trees of about 70 years make up the major part of the forest, forming a light-proof canopy which kills all other plants

Ranks of English archers, with their 'unchivalrous' yew longbows, were used in battle to set up formidable artillery-type barrages that weakened the enemy in preparation for infantry or cavalry offences by the 'nobility'

and discourages birds – hence the phrase birdless groves, sometimes used to describe yew woods. Also within the reserve is a circular two-mile nature trail affording open views as it crosses airy downland which supports a rich flora and fauna.

The nearest car park to Kingley Vale is not marked or sign-posted, but can be found at the beginning of a mile-long access path to the reserve entrance (see also page 21).

Fulking's Shepherd and Dog pub is a reminder that the village once depended for its living on the thousands of sheep that grazed the high downland escarpment above it

Fletching

Map Ref: 87TQ4223

This small village has two pubs, two shops, a church and a school, and lies just off the main A272 north of Uckfield. It is not a place that people come through to get somewhere else, though there was one notable exception in 1264, when Simon de Montfort camped with his army in the forest round the village on his way to fight the Battle of Lewes the next day. From that engagement grew the English parliament of today.

De Montfort himself kept vigil with his knights in the little village church, which had been completed only 34 years earlier – though the tower is even older – and legend has it that a number of his favourite knights slain in the battle were carried back to Fletching and buried in full armour beneath the nave.

The slender spire can be seen for miles around, and there is a mausoleum housing the remains of the 1st Earl of Sheffield and his family. There too is buried Edward Gibbon who wrote *The Decline and Fall of the Roman Empire* at nearby Sheffield Park. The timber-framed cottages that line parts of the High Street date from the 15th and 17th centuries, but those opposite the church were built in Victorian times. The rather strange Gothic turreted castle gateway leads into Sheffield Park (see page 63).

Friston

Map Ref: 87TV5598

Friston, on the top of a hill between the Cuckmere Valley and East Dean, has a church, a pond, a Tudor manor house and a forest named after it – but there is no village. The church stands quite alone beside a pond, the oldest part dating from 1042, and inside can be found a practical guide sheet giving just the kind of information a casual visitor wants to know: the age of the church and everything in it, and the origins of the graffiti scrawled on the rough chalk in the old porch. A notice suggests this to be 'the results of the visits of a certain class possessed of a knife and itching fingers'. The church door is dedicated to the memory of composer Frank Bridge, Benjamin Britten's first teacher.

An unmade road alongside the church affords sweeping views towards the Seven Sisters, and in the nearby hamlet of Crowlink the cellars under Crowlink House are said to have contained the 'Genuine Crowling', a smuggled gin worth a lot of money in the 19th century.

In Friston Forest are circular walks through woodlands planted by the Forestry Commission; descriptive leaflets are available at Seven Sisters Country Park Centre, Exceat (see page 45).

Fulking

Map Ref: 86TQ2411

Well before the 19th century, when the Downs had more sheep than there were people in the hamlets and farms below, many downland villages in the late spring would send their sheep to Fulking for washing before the annual sheep-shearing. They were driven to a stream which runs down to the main road from the steep escarpment of the Downs, and washed in the dammed up watercourse. The road was closed to such traffic as existed, with temporary gates at each end.

Conveniently near by stood the Shepherd and Dog Inn, and at the end of each day's work it would be filled with the shepherds in their smocks, smoking long clay pipes while they relaxed over their pints, their dogs at their feet. Then it would be the turn of the shearing gangs, who would meet in the inn for their pay and a meal when their work was completed.

Nowadays, the stream is channelled through a Victorian well-house beside the road, displaying a suitably grateful tiled text.

Entrance to the churchyard at Friston is by a gate that pivots on a central pole – a type peculiar to Sussex and not particularly common even there

Fine knapped-flint work is a feature of 16th-century Glynde Place, which was remodelled in the 18th century

Parading prior to a race at Goodwood

Goodwood gained a grandstand in 1842

Glynde

Map Ref: 87TQ4509

This small village is at the foot of Mount Caburn, near Ringmer, and has a great house, an ancient church and a long grassy bank covered in spring with hundreds of daffodils.

Glynde Place – with its high yew hedges, imposing gateways, courtyards and portrait-hung Long Gallery – is an Elizabethan manor that has belonged to only three families in 400 years. The church alongside it (once its chapel) was built in 1765 by a member of one of them, a certain Richard Trevor, who was Bishop of Durham, to a design by Sir Thomas Robinson. Sir Thomas had just returned from Italy full of enthusiasm for Renaissance architecture, and decided to apply the latest designs to his church at Glynde. The result is a rectangular building of knapped flint, with a coved rococo ceiling, box pews and a gallery that was described in 1852 by one writer as 'in very bad taste'. The walls are rather strangely covered in a blue and brown brocaded linen.

Glynde's most famous inhabitant was John Ellman (1753–1832), who bred the black-faced Southdown sheep. He was a benevolent farmer who lodged all his unmarried labourers under his own roof and, when they married, gave them a pig, a cow and some grassland of their own. He also built a school for their children. But he would not allow a licenced house in Glynde. It did not matter if his men drank beer, but he apparently liked them to brew it at home. Glyndebourne Opera House lies in Ringmer (see pages 60–61).

Goodwood

Map Ref: 84SU8808

Goodwood's history is one of addition, embellishment and care – but in order to survive, it now has to be run on business lines under a trusteeship led by the Earl of March, whose family – the Dukes of Richmond – has owned the house since 1697. Charles Lennox – the 1st Duke – was the natural

THE NEW GRAND STAND AT GOODWOOD.

son of Charles II and his mistress, the French emissary Louise de Kerouaille. The Jacobean house he bought as a hunting lodge passed to the 2nd Duke, who built Carné's Seat – a stone temple from which there are marvellous views. Near by is The Trundle, another high point and the site of a pre-Roman hillfort.

The present flint house, which was designed by James Wyatt at the end of the 1700s, was built by the 3rd Duke – who also enlarged the estate and planted cedars of Lebanon and cork oaks, some of which still stand. The elegant state apartments contain such priceless treasures as Gobelin tapestries, Louis XV furniture and Sèvres china, mostly bought by the 3rd Duke when he was Ambassador to the Court of Louis XV at Versailles. Other intriguing relics include a shirt belonging to Charles I, and Napoleon's chair.

The world-famous Goodwood racecourse was laid out on top of the Downs by the 3rd Duke and enlarged by the 5th, who gave racing its prestige in the mid-1800s. Luxurious kennels built for Goodwood Hunt now house a golf club, and the old Richmond Arms coaching inn has been transformed into a 50-bedroom hotel. Other estate businesses are: the famous motor racing circuit, now used for car testing, trials and rallies; an airfield with flying club; a school; an air-taxi service; horse trials and dressage championships; farming and forestry; a touring caravan site; and a country park.

AA recommends:
Hotel: Goodwood Park, 3-star, *tel.* (0243) 775537
Campsite: Goodwood Racecourse (TRAX) Caravan Club Site, 2-pennants, *tel.* (0243) 774486

Halland

Map Ref: 87TQ5016

Bentley Wildfowl Collection and Motor Museum provides something for all the family. Over 1,000 species of swans, geese and flamingoes can be seen on the lakes and streams in the beautiful grounds of Bentley House. The Motor Museum shows the development of motoring, and has vintage Edwardian and veteran vehicles. There is also a formal garden, a woodland walk, a craft barn and a gift shop, plus a childrens' play area and places set aside for picnics. In the house itself is a splendid collection of antique furniture.

AA recommends:
Hotel: Halland Forge, 2-star, *tel.* (082584) 456

Hamsey

Map Ref: 87TQ4112

In 925 King Athelstan held a meeting of his counsellors in a manor house at Hamsey – which suggests that it must have been a place of some importance – but today only the little medieval church, remote and quiet, remains. It stands off the A275 just north of Lewes, beyond a canal bridge and through a farmyard. All around are the flat lands of the Ouse Valley, and in the churchyard brown shaggy sheep keep the grass short. The church, which was completely neglected in the 19th century and restored in the 1920s, is kept locked – but the key can be found at the village shop.

Close by is the village of Offham, where on the Downs above in 1264 Simon de Montfort defeated Henry III. As a result the *Mise of Lewes* was drawn up, which is often referred to as the origin of English parliamentary government. The village has a country house, some flint cottages, a pub and a 19th-century church – plus one of the cottages are thatched and timber-framed, and it was described by E V Lucas as 'perhaps the most satisfying village in all Sussex'. Its 14th-century church of St Mary and St Gabriel is larger than many, and in the churchyard features a war memorial by Eric Gill – along with many 18th-century headstones. There too are the old village stocks, used as late as 1860, and a whipping post with iron wrist cuffs at different heights.

Inside the church is a memorial in the chancel to the colourful Sir Henry Featherstonehaugh of Uppark, who died in 1846 (see page 68). H D Gordon, rector at South Harting for many years, wrote a gossipy and entertaining history of the parish in 1877. In it he included excerpts from letters in which the Lady Caryll writes of her steward's wife (whom she much disliked), as being 'sick of the mulygrubes'. This mysterious illness was less comic than it sounds, since the poor soul died soon afterwards.

South Harting's Early English cruciform church is distinguished by a soaring, copper-clad broach spire

elevated position on a sandy ridge between former forest in the north and the often-flooded brooklands of the River Adur in the south and east. A moated medieval site discovered near by has yielded several artefacts, which are housed in Henfield's interesting little museum. They include a slab of fossiliferous Sussex marble, which is also known locally as winkle stone (see page 24).

Once a centre for lime-burning, the village supplied lime for 'marling' or 'sweetening' the clay fields of the Weald, and mortar for building before cement was known. Kilns at Upper Beeding were the forerunners of the present-day Beeding Cement Works.

An 18th-century water-mill south of Henfield near the hamlet of Small Dole, on the A2037, is the site for the headquarters of the Sussex Trust for Nature Conservation. Including a nature reserve and countryside exhibition, it offers an astonishing variety of things to see and do in the comparatively small space of 15 acres. The trail around the woodland, marsh and streams is

first 'railways' in southern England. Operated in 1809, it consisted of wagons attached to cables and worked on a funicular basis through two brick tunnels under the road, carrying chalk and lime to the canal 400ft below. The tunnels by the Chalk Pit pub can still be seen.

Hartings, The

Map Ref: 84SU7819

Main village of three grouped close together, South Harting – the one with the church – lies under the Downs near the Hampshire border and seems to be more of that county than of Sussex. Some of its

Henfield

Map Ref: 86TQ2116

The Cat House – a pretty, 16th-century thatched cottage near the church – has a procession of wrought-iron cats, with paws stretched to birds, following each other round the eaves. It is said they were the owner's comment on the vicar's cat catching his canary. Also, there is an 18th-century Sun Insurance firemark medallion over the front door, which identified which insurance company brigade should be called on in the event of a domestic fire.

Henfield's Anglo-Saxon name of Hamefelde describes the manor's

splendidly planned, and there is a dipping pond where children may net and identify specimens (nets provided). The mill machinery is restored, there is a vivarium for harvest mice and also an aquarium. Audio-visual displays are installed too. Various courses and other special activities are held throughout the season for adults and children. The attractive gift counter is open during the autumn for Christmas shopping.

AA recommends:
Guesthouse: Great Wapses, Wineham (farmhouse), *tel.* (0273) 492544, (3m NE off B2116)
Campsite: Downsview Caravan Park, Bramlands La, Woodmancote, 2-pennants, *tel.* (0273) 492801

Herstmonceux

Map Ref: 87TQ6312

Beautiful red-brick and moated 15th-century Herstmonceux (pronounced Hurstmonsoo) Castle has long been known as the home of the Science and Engineering Research Council's Royal Greenwich Observatory, with a Visitor Centre displaying wonders of the universe ranging from the discoveries of Isaac Newton to black holes in space. Opposite the entrance to the castle is the parish church, with a 12th-century tower and on the floor a canopied brass to Sir William Fiennes – whose son Roger built the stronghold.

Two miles away in the village can be bought trugs, which are oval-shaped baskets of willow and sweet chestnut that can be used for anything from fruit and eggs to logs. They have been made in Herstmonceux for over 200 years, but became nationally known when a certain Thomas Smith displayed

Trug making in the original Victorian manner is still a going concern at The Royal Sussex Trug Shop, and the Truggery, in Herstmonceux village

them at the Great Exhibition of 1851. Queen Victoria ordered several, and Thomas walked from Herstmonceux to London and back to deliver them personally. His company, the Royal Sussex Trug Shop, was founded in 1828 and some of his descendants still work there. Farther down the road is the weather-boarded cottage of The Truggery, where three generations of the Reed family once worked.

The village has a good variety of pubs. The Woolpack, once a coaching inn, was where local farmers took their wool after shearing; The Welcome Stranger is one of the smallest inns in Sussex, and was named to commemorate the birth of an heir to the lord of the manor; and the 17th-century Brewers Arms preserves a good example of Sussex timber-boarding.

AA recommends:
Restaurant: Sundial, 2-fork, 1-rosette, *tel.* (0323) 832217
Guesthouse: Cleavers Lyng Country Hotel, Church Rd, *tel.* (0323) 833131

Saxon Churches

Well established a century before the Norman invasion, the development of the parish church in England can be traced from at least the 8th century, despite the fact that most Saxon churches, minsters and monasteries were built of wood and have been lost. Often they were destroyed, rebuilt and destroyed again during the Viking raids of the 9th century, but the Normans for their own reasons were also great despoilers, razing important buildings and rebuilding on the same foundations.

What survived were smaller, stone-built structures, of which the South Downs region has a surprisingly high number. It has been calculated that 60 churches in Sussex possess some Saxon stone – or even Roman bricks reclaimed by economical builders! With a few exceptions, of which St Botolph's near Hardham is one, they reflect the Kentish form of building, based on a simplified basilican plan. In the other great centre of Saxon churches, Northumbria, the builders worked to a distinctly Celtic plan – tall, narrow naves and rectangular chancels. St Botolph's is of this Northumbrian form.

Bishopstone has perhaps the area's finest representative of the golden age of Saxon church architecture, giving the lie to the theory that the Saxons were uncouth, and that the country was only civilised under the Normans.

Woolbeding church preserves Saxon work in its decorative stone pilaster stripes, which are similar to those gracing the tower at Sompting, perhaps the most famous Saxon church in the county. This

notable survival has remained unaltered since it was built nearly 1,000 years ago, and the pyramidal Rhenish helm with which it is capped has been the subject of innumerable illustrations in architectural textbooks. Unique in Britain, it is of a timbered and gabled construction that seems more appropriate to the Rhine Valley than to a Sussex village.

Although not as impressive as Sompting, other Sussex churches preserve interesting examples of pre-Norman work. For instance, the charming shoreline village of Bosham has a church in which part of the chancel is of Saxon date. Chithurst's has an aisleless nave and Clayton's is of a design in which there are many early features.

Once the eye has become accustomed to such features they can be recognised in churches throughout the South Downs region, ranging from single carved stones to complete arches.

St Andrew's at Bishopstone (below) is of Saxon origin but has Norman features too, like the carved arch above

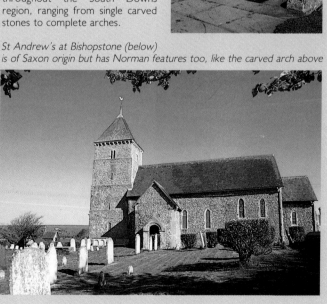

Hurstpierpoint

Map Ref: 86TQ2816

Close to the line of Roman Stane Street, this handsome Georgian development has a church by Charles Barry – architect of the Houses of Parliament – which incorporates monuments from its medieval predecessor. However, the village is better known for the public school of Hurstpierpoint College, and the splendid Elizabethan manor house of Danny, which stands in a fine park near by.

Danny was built by George Goring on an estate granted by Queen Elizabeth I, and in gratitude for her largesse he designed the house in the shape of the letter 'E'. Subsequently it passed into the Campion family, who added a wing during the reign of Queen Anne, and in 1918 was the meeting place of the War Cabinet under Prime Minister Lloyd George. Armistice with Germany was signed there.

In pleasant gardens not far from Danny stands Newtimber Place, a moated 17th-century house known for its Etruscan-style frescoes. Just south at Newtimber Hill are 238 acres of National Trust downland.

AA recommends:
Restaurant: Barrons, 120 High St, Hassocks, 1-fork, *tel.* (0273) 832183

Newtimber Place, near Hurstpierpoint, dates from 1680 but the site has been occupied since Norman times

Itchenor

Map Ref: 84SU7901

In the 13th century – when the people of the hamlet which succeeded the Saxon settlement of Icenore built a church – they chose St Nicholas, the guardian of seafarers, as their patron. The same small stone building is now the parish church of Itchenor.

A shipyard established there in the early 1600s ended with the building of minesweepers during the last war. St Nicholas was well-chosen, however, for today Itchenor is heavily involved in sailing and yachting, and has a yard building glass-fibre hulls. The single street leads to the shore, there is a pub and a ship's chandler – but there is no shop.

Small though it is, Itchenor is the customs-clearance port for the whole of Chichester Harbour, and is the home of the Chichester Harbour Conservancy. A small-boat ferry service for foot passengers connects with Bosham, and for the many non-sailing visitors who find their way down to this little port in the summer there is the *Wingate II* – a 70-seater traditional passenger boat – which makes the same trip.

Jevington

Map Ref: 87TQ5601

About the time Alfred the Great was fighting the Danes, a Saxon by the name of Jeva obtained land for his tribe in a hollow of the chalk downland near Eastbourne, and

---

The Rapes of Sussex

Historically there are five Rapes of Sussex – the term 'rape' being an Anglo-Saxon word of imprecise definition, used to describe strategic areas that served as units of local government within individual kingdoms. This practice of dividing the land began during the Anglo-Saxon settlements, and the Rapes of Sussex – along with their counterparts, the Lathes of Kent – are probably the earliest examples. Each had a court in which administration was discussed and disputes resolved.

Under Edward the Confessor local government was further rationalised with the introduction of the shires. They in turn were divided into hundreds, which absorbed the old Rapes, Lathes and similar units. However, after the Conquest William I immediately recognised the strategic importance of the older divisions – each of which contained a seaport, or a river which coincided with a gap in the Downs – and gave them to supporters in reward for their loyalty. In this way he ensured their continued fidelity while guaranteeing safe passage to the coast of his new English kingdom and access to his Normandy Dukedom.

Under their new owners, each of the Rapes soon gained a strong castle that served the dual purpose of subjugating the local Anglo-Saxon farmers and forming a powerful

The 13th-century towers of 11th-century Lewes Castle, which blocked a narrow pass through the Downs

deterrent to would-be invaders approaching from England's southern shores.

Perhaps the finest of these great Norman fortifications, and certainly the best preserved, is at Arundel. Looming above the water meadows of the River Arun, it developed to its present rambling proportions from a castle built soon after the Conquest by the noble Roger of Montgomery.

In complete contrast is ruined Bramber, of which only a stark, obelisk-like fragment remains on the mound where William of Briouze built his great castle to guard the River Adur route inland from the sea.

Also high on a motte and visible from most places in and around the town are the more extensive ruins of Lewes Castle, which was built by William of Warenne to defend the River Ouse and its wide, flat flood plain. Among the remains survives a good amount of Norman architecture.

Pevensey Castle, built by the Count of Mortain within Roman walls, stands near the spot where the Conquerer landed with his invading army. It has a long and bitter military history that reaches clear from the 12th century to 1940, when it was refortified against the threat of yet another invasion.

The fortification built at Hastings by the Count of Eu once held a commanding position high above the sea, but the very suitability of that site has proved its undoing. The cliff edge which formed such an excellent defence has been in constant retreat over the centuries, and the ruins cling precariously to land that is destined for the sea.

Jevington was established. In the 18th century the village was a popular place for smugglers, who brought their booty across the valley from Crowlink and Birling Gap to store it in the cellars of the Rectory, whose walls still bear arrow marks left by the excise men. The gang's headquarters was the local inn (now the Hungry Monk restaurant) which had a landlord who was ringleader of a group of highwaymen and smugglers until he was hanged in 1796.

Starting at Jevington is a footpath that leads some three miles to Alfriston

Cowslips flourish among many other wild flowers in the Jevington meadows

through locally-named Onion Wood – because of the wild garlic growing there. Winding lanes once used by pilgrims lead to Monastery Field, with its foundations of a 14th-century settlement, past woods with badger setts and over meadows where cowslips and orchids grow.

AA recommends:
Restaurant: Hungry Monk, 2-fork, *tel.* (03212) 2178

Lewes

Map Ref: 87TQ4110

Lewes is an ancient and historic town with an 11th-century castle and 14th-century Barbican Gate. It has a 300-year-old bowling green that was once the scene of medieval jousting, various old churches, and museums and art galleries. There are book and antique shops to browse in, peaceful gardens to sit in, friendly pubs and excellent restaurants. Fifteenth-century timbered cottages rub shoulders with elegant Georgian houses, and colour-washed walls.

The best way to see the town for the first time is to climb to the top of the castle that William de Warenne built in 1067. From there can be seen an attractive jumble of red roofs and neat cottages, with Offham Hill – where in 1264 Simon de Montfort defeated Henry III – to the west, and Mount

Caburn and Firle Beacon to the east. Through the flat fields beyond, the River Ouse meanders to the sea.

The main street stretches from one end of the town to the other along the line of an ancient causeway, with medieval passages winding beneath chunks of the old flint town wall. There is Keere Street, down whose steep cobbles George IV (then Prince Regent) is said to have driven his coach and four for a bet; Pipe Passage, the town sentry's night walk in the Middle Ages; and narrow English Passage, which separates cottages from their own front gardens.

Tom Paine, who did so much to inspire the American War of Independence, lived here at Bull House (now a restaurant); so did Gideon Mantell, the early 19th-century geologist and expert on dinosaurs; and John Harvard, who married a local girl in South Malling Church in 1636 and later founded the American university. The most visited house today is that known as Anne of Cleves' who – ironically – never actually lived in Lewes. The 16th-century timber-framed building is worth seeing for its contents alone, a fascinating collection of iron and stone work, medieval furniture and relics from the town's sometimes turbulent past.

Seventeen Protestant martyrs imprisoned in the cellars of the old Star Inn, now the Town Hall, and burnt at the stake in the street above, are remembered every 5

Cobbled Keere Street, the oldest thoroughfare in Lewes, runs along the line of a medieval town-boundary ditch

November when Lewes holds its famous Bonfire Night celebrations. People pour in from neighbouring towns and villages to watch the brilliantly costumed figures with their 5,000 flaming torches march down the winding High Street.

AA recommends:
Hotels: Shelley's, High St, 3-star, *tel.* (0273) 472361
White Hart, High St, 2-star, *tel.* (0273) 474676
Restaurant: Kenwards, Pipe Passage, 151A High St, 1-fork, *tel.* (0273) 472343
Self Catering: 19A Cliffe High St, *tel.* (0273) 507381
Leigh Cottage, 37 Southover High St, Southover, *tel.* (0273) 514484
Garages: Market Lane, Units 1 & 8, Cliffe Ind Est, *tel.* (0273) 477744
Caffyns, Brooks Rd, *tel.* (0273) 473186
Morris Road, Morris Rd, *tel.* (0273) 472434

Good fish-scale tile hanging in Lewes

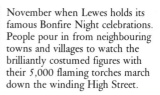

Lindfield

Map Ref: 86TQ3425

One of those picture-book villages that give people living abroad instant nostalgia for England, Lindfield has an ancient church at one end – and at the other a pond with waterfowl, a tiny island, and gardens sloping down to the water's edge. Between is an immaculately-groomed High Street, with colour-washed Georgian and timber-framed houses, giant magnolia trees, flowering cherries and camellias in the front gardens. Lime trees that once gave the village its name (the Anglo-Saxon word *lind* means lime) edge the street that used to be an important stopping place for horse-drawn stagecoaches on the London-to-Brighton route. Two of the hostelries they used, The Red Lion and The Bent Arms, remain, but The Tiger is now a church house – though the owners have retained the inn sign outside. The old Toll House is a dress shop.

The medieval church has an unusual two-storied porch, a tall spire and parish records that go back to 765. In 1150 Lindfield was granted to the College of South Malling near Lewes, and Malling Priory – a Georgian House in the High Street – commemorates this. In 1344 Edward III granted Lindfield a weekly market and the right to hold two annual fairs. The August Sheep Fair, once famous throughout the south, is held no longer. There is, however, still an annual summer fair.

Around the church are some of the most beautiful houses in the country, with 15th-century Church Cottage and the gabled and timber-framed Old Place – with its mullioned windows – dating from about 1590. The village, once a centre for making candles, gloves and pianos, has always been associated with the Quakers; William Allen (1770 to 1843), who did so much for prison reform and the abolition of slavery, lived there.

Two examples from a wealth of fine buildings represent Lindfield's exceptional domestic architecture

Litlington

Map Ref: 87TQ5201

This village – between wooded downland and water meadows, four miles from Seaford on the left bank of the Cuckmere River – can have changed little over the last 100 years, and has Saxon origins. The first known rector, a certain John Rede, of the little flint church of St Michael the Archangel was installed in 1374, though the date of the original building is about 1150. Outside is a 13th-century sundial on the wall of the porch, and two more on the north-west buttress.

On the other side of the road up a wooded drive is Clapham House, now a cookery school, but once said to have been the home of Mrs Fitzherbert, to whom George IV would ride from Brighton.

A place to which many generations have returned since it opened 100 years ago is the Litlington Tea House, with its Pleasure Gardens. Secluded grassy terraces are shielded by ancient trees which cut off the noise of traffic from the road below. There is also a large nursery selling plants, pots and garden furniture. From Litlington can be seen the 90ft-long White Horse that was cut into Windover Hill in the 1920s.

Tea at Litlington is a genteel affair

Littlehampton

Map Ref: 85TQ0202

Although it never reached the heights of Regency fashion or architectural grace that Brighton and Worthing did, this Arun-mouth town has received its own measure of popularity as a resort – and continues to do so. A charming feature is the extensive green, which forms a wide buffer between the seafront and the first houses.

Facing both the River Arun and the sea is a large amusement

Formative days of a seaside resort, captured in a painting displayed at the Littlehampton Maritime Museum

complex, much of which is under cover, while upstream near the town's old swingbridge – long-defunct – is a boating marina from which local skippers operate fishing trips. Although Littlehampton no longer has the considerable status as a port that it once enjoyed, a scattering of old riverside sheds and warehouses are reminders that trade continued until quite recently.

Attractions include the Pleasure Grounds, with tennis courts, bowling greens, and the like. Crazy golf and similar excitements are found along the front, and there is a good local museum in River Road.

About a mile inland and close to a wide meander of the River Arun is Climping, which is built around a church that is well known for its original architecture. Perhaps the most complete example of its type to have survived in Britain, it preserves a trans-Norman tower with 4ft-thick walls of Caen stone and 10 mass dials.

AA recommends:
Hotel: Bailiffscourt, 3-star, country-house, *tel.* (0903) 723511
Guesthouses: Old Windmill House, 83 South Ter, *tel.* (0903) 724939
Regency Hotel, 85 South Ter, *tel.* (0903) 717707
Self Catering: Canadian Village, Rope Walk (chalets), *tel.* (0903) 713816
Campsite: White Rose Touring Park, Mill La, Wick, 3-pennants, *tel.* (0903) 716176
Garages: Cuff Miller, Horsham Rd, *tel.* (0903) 714367
Rowes, Terminus Rd, *tel.* (0903) 717271

Mardens, The

Map Ref: 84SU7713

West Marden is the largest of four hamlets carrying the name, and is the only one without a church. Situated on the B2146 Chichester–Harting road, it comprises a few flintstone cottages climbing prettily up a hill, an inn, a weeping willow – and views of the Downs. East Marden has a handful of old flint-and-tile cottages grouped round a tiny village green, hardly big enough to take the thatched well-head which stands at its centre, under the guardianship of 13th-century St Peter's Church.

Up Marden has two or three farms on a 500ft ridge near Stoughton, and its church of St Michael is one of the most remote in southern England. It has received little attention in 300 years, and its 13th-century structure survives with not a window altered. It is thought to have been a resting-place on the pilgrim route from Winchester to Chichester.

North Marden is even more isolated, and its Norman Church of St Mary – reached by a footpath through a farmyard – is all there is of it. One of the smallest in Sussex, St Mary's is one of Kipling's 'little, lost Down churches' and is mentioned in 13th-century records. Its simple rectangular form is broken by an unusual apsidal – or semi-circular chancel end – and it has a square bell tower. Built of Caen stone which was probably shipped from Normandy to Chichester, St Mary's is open for services only at Easter and Thanksgiving.

Mayfield

Map Ref: 87TQ5826

This exceptionally-pretty 1,000-year-old village has a main street lined with a variety of lovely buildings. From the top can be seen timber-framing, white weather-boarding, gabled roofs, stonework and overhanging tiles.

St Dunstan, who is said to have built Mayfield's first wooden church in AD960, is also reputed to have founded the adjacent Palace of the Archbishop of Canterbury – where Sir Thomas Gresham, keeper of the Privy Purse and founder of the London Stock Exchange, entertained Queen Elizabeth I in the 1570s. The building is now a Roman Catholic boarding school for girls and the great hall is now the college chapel. Dominating the High Street is the timber-framed Middle House, built in 1575 for Sir Thomas Gresham.

The unusually elaborate village sign that won second prize in a national newspaper competition in 1920 shows a young woman, and children with flowers. Beneath it is a suggestion for the derivation of the name Mayfield – that it comes from Magfild, meaning maid's field. The village was the centre of the Sussex iron trade until the 18th century, and a local rhyme says: 'Master Huggett and his man John, They did cast the first cannon.'

AA recommends:
Restaurant: Old Brew House, High St, 1-fork, *tel.* (0435) 872342

Mayfield High Street, earlier this century; little has changed, and the fine weatherboarding remains intact

Church and Devil tussle for supremacy, while children bear flowers in the 'maid's field' of Mayfield's sign

Michelham Priory

Map Ref: 87TQ5609

The first sound that greets the visitor to this beautiful medieval priory is of running water by the mill, and the quack of ducks on the encircling moat. The mill, first mentioned in 1434, has been restored and visitors can watch the French burr millstone grinding Sussex wheat into wholemeal flour, while having the whole process explained by a helpful guide.

Something of the peaceful nature of the monks themselves seems to permeate the Augustinian Priory, which was founded in 1229 and features a 14th-century gateway over the moat. The church was destroyed at the Dissolution of the Monasteries in the 16th century, and in 1587 the Pelham family converted the refectory and added another wing.

Today it is a happy place for young and old to visit. Outside, as well as the interesting water-mill, is a Physic Garden with plants that would have been used medicinally in medieval times; excellent notices explain which plants would have been used for which complaint. Also of interest are a magnificent 17th-century Tudor barn, a forge, a wheelwright's shop, a rope-making museum, a restaurant and a shop for craft and guide books.

Inside, there is beautiful 14th-century stone vaulting in the entrance hall, plus furniture, tapestries, pictures and an intriguing display of musical instruments including miniature guitars and lutes from Italy, and flutes from Jugoslavia, Mexico and Japan. The original 16th-century kitchen has a sandstone chimney, and there is a Tudor Room with chests, stools and an oak refectory table laid with pewter mugs and plates. An irresistible dolls' house is packed with items, some of which – like the tiny gramophone record that plays the National Anthem – are duplicates from Queen Mary's.

Midhurst

Map Ref: 84SU8821

If its Saxon name is to be believed, this ancient and picturesque market town was once surrounded by forest. The wildwood has gone, but the River Rother which supplied water and grinding power remains – as do many fine old buildings from various periods. In Knockhundred Row a 17th-century cottage now houses the public library, and close by in the Market Square is timber-framed Elizabeth House, featuring a 16th-century mural.

Market Hall was built in 1552 and housed the town's first grammar school. Most of the parish church dates from the 19th century, although 13th-century work can be seen in the tower and there are 16th-century features elsewhere. Prominent in South Street is the Spread Eagle Inn, which dates from coaching days and features a front of about 1700. A timbered and overhanging section of the building is claimed to be 15th-century.

The name Midhurst is synonymous with Cowdray Park, and just past the end of the main street is a causeway – slightly higher than old flood-water levels – which leads to the ruins of one of Tudor England's most magnificent fortified manor houses. Built by the Earl of Southampton in the first half of the 16th century, the house burnt

A fine Tudor mansion incorporating extensive remains of the original 13th-century Michelham Priory houses displays of artefacts owned by the Sussex Archaeological Society

Polo grounds, much patronised by royalty, at Cowdray Park. The game is also played on Ambersham Common

down in 1793 and early this century passed into the hands of the 1st Viscount Cowdray of Midhurst. For some generations it was the home of the Viscounts Montague. Exhibits relating to the estate and its owners can be seen in the Cowdray Museum. The 600-acre Cowdray Park is famous for its polo grounds.

AA recommends:
Hotels: Spread Eagle, South St, 3-star, *tel.* (073081) 2211
Angel, North St, 2-star, *tel.* (073081) 2421
Restaurant: Olde Manor House, Church Hill, 2-fork, *tel.* (073081) 2990
Garage: Midhurst Eng & Mtr, Rumbolds Hill, *tel.* (073081) 2162

Literary Figures

Rudyard Kipling's poem about the 'blunt, bow-headed, whale-backed Downs' was just one expression of his love for that landscape. From 1897 until 1902 he lived at Rottingdean, then moved to Bateman's near Burwash on the Sussex Weald. Kipling's affection for the area was matched by that of Hilaire Belloc, who wrote a passionate poem about the decay of agriculture in England, comparing it with the ruin of Halnaker Mill (which was later saved). Belloc lived in Slindon during his childhood and again, briefly, when married. He too settled in a Wealden village, Shipley.

Anthony Trollope lived at South Harting from 1880–2, about the same time as the young H G Wells left nearby Uppark, where his mother was housekeeper, to become an apprentice draper at Portsmouth. John Galsworthy spent working holidays at Littlehampton and later lived at Bury, where his ashes were scattered. H E Bates wrote many of his best-known short stories while stationed at RAF Tangmere (now an aviation museum, see page 40), during World War II.

Virginia and Leonard Woolf spent much of their married life in Sussex, first leasing a reputedly-haunted

Rudyard Kipling lived at Rottingdean before moving to Burwash in 1902

Anthony Trollope

Regency–Gothic house in Asheham, near Lewes which Virginia described in her book *A Haunted House*. In 1919 they bought 18th-century Monk's House at Rodmell, close to the River Ouse where Virginia drowned herself in 1941. Leonard continued to live there until 1969. The Woolfs were key figures of the 'Bloomsbury' set – a close-knit intellectual élite – as were Virginia's sister Vanessa Bell, her husband Clive and Duncan Grant, who also made Sussex their home when they bought Charleston Farmhouse near Firle in 1916. Among the distinguished literary and artistic visitors to the two households were T S Eliot, E M Forster, Roger Fry and Lytton Strachey.

Among poets connected with the Downs are the sonnet-writer Charlotte Smith; William Blake, who lived briefly at Felpham and while there composed *Jerusalem* and W B Yeats, who often stayed at the Chantry House at Steyning.

Of all the writers who have lived on or near the Downs over the centuries, perhaps the naturalist Richard Jefferies – who spent the last years of his life at Goring-by-Sea – expressed his feelings the most poignantly. An outsider like Kipling and the irrepressible Belloc, his writing nevertheless unfailingly catches the spirit of the land he grew to appreciate so much.

Newhaven

Map Ref: 87TQ4401

About 400 years ago a storm caused the River Ouse to change course, and Newhaven was built to replace the blocked harbour at Seaford. Today it is a busy port, and the start of a four-hour ferry crossing to Dieppe. It also has a sandy beach and the fascinating Newhaven and Seaford Historical Society Museum – started by Peter Bailey, who had collected so many photographs about Newhaven and the cross-Channel ferries he decided to open a Museum. Now run by volunteers, it is only open afternoons on Saturdays, and Bank holidays.

A roadside notice just outside the town encourages visitors to stop at the 12th-century parish church, but after climbing the path to get to it they may find another notice saying it has to be locked from time to time. The key can normally be obtained from the rector, who lives 10yds from the entrance. A Marina Coastal Path is being restored and a Valley Ponds conservation project is under way near the town. Sadly, Newhaven Fort – built in the 1860s and opened in 1982 as a tourist attraction – had to close down; its future is uncertain.

The 17th-century Bridge Hotel was a refuge for Louis Phillipe on his escape from the French uprising in 1848.

AA recommends:

Self Catering: The Granary (flats), for bookings Mrs B M Cheeseman, High Barn, Piddinghoe, *tel.* (0273) 514484

Newick

Map Ref: 87TQ4121

At the centre of this village is a triangular green with a pump dating from 1897, the year of Queen Victoria's Diamond Jubilee. A useful map here shows the locations of interesting local buildings, among which is School Cottage – where in the 1770s Lady Vernon educated 12 poor girls in reading, writing and needlework to make them 'useful servants'. She also founded a Trust, which still exists – though not for

the same purpose!

Parts of the church date from Norman times and inside is a Jacobean pulpit with a sounding board. A pitch pipe in the tower was used by the choir until 1860.

About a mile south of the village on the Barcombe road is Newick Park, an 18th-century country mansion set in over 200 acres of gardens, park and farmland – now the home of Lord and Lady Brentford. The gardens are renowned. Just north of The Dell area – with its rare trees and shrubs – is the walled Sifelle Nursery, where herbs and flowers are sold.

Newhaven, the only Sussex Channel port of importance in Sussex, narrowly escaped becoming the 'Liverpool of the South' in Victorian times

Parham

Map Ref: 85TQ0614

This splendid Elizabethan mansion
stands in a deer park among great
trees, statues and a lake in a
beautiful downland setting. Dating
from 1577, Parham House has
been continuously occupied by
three successive families. Their latest
descendant still lives there, which
no doubt contributes to the friendly
atmosphere of the house.

The main room is the magnificent
Great Hall, overlooked through
internal mullioned windows by the
Steward's Room. Its other principal
room, on the top floor, is the Long
Gallery. At nearly 160ft this is one
of the longest in the country, and
has superb views over the park. The
ceiling is a contemporary design by
Oliver Messel, which fits in well
with the original oak wainscoting
and floor. In Tudor times Long
Galleries were used for exercise and
children's games.

Parham contains over 300
Elizabethan and Stuart paintings,
including Zucchero's famous
portrait of Elizabeth I. Equally
important is 'arguably the finest
collection of needlework in any
house in England'. The most
impressive is the Great Bed, with its
incredible silk embroidered hangings
worked in the 16th and early 17th
centuries.

The gardens were redesigned in
1982, with herbaceous borders,
herb garden and an orchard.
Children can still explore the
Wendy house built into one of the
surrounding old walls. Refreshments
are served in the Big Kitchen.

Petersfield

Map Ref: 84SU7423

Scattered among the Georgian and
neo-Georgian architecture of
comparatively recent years are clues
of a long history that extends back
at least to the town's first charter in
the 12th century. It was about that
time when the Church of St Peter
was built, and despite 19th-century
restoration it retains a fine Norman
nave, separated from the chancel by
a contemporary arch which is all
that remains of a long-vanished
central tower.

From medieval times until the last
century Petersfield was a prosperous
centre of the wool and leather
trades, and during the coaching era
the town and its nine inns hosted
nearly 30 vehicles each day.
Notable old buildings survive in
Sheep Street, Dragon Street and
College Street, and an area called
The Spain is thought to have been
named after Spanish wool
merchants who traded there.

A little to the south of the town
is the 80-acre Petersfield Heath,
which has a lake and no fewer than
21 prehistoric barrows.

AA recommends:
Guesthouse: Concorde Hotel, 1 Weston
Rd, *tel.* (0730) 63442

*Parham's Great Hall is noted for the
fine plasterwork of its ceiling, and
mullioned windows of unusual height*

*Petworth appears to have a central
tower when viewed from the western
aspect, but the feature belongs to St
Mary's Church, which is on the other
side of the house*

Petworth

Map Ref: 85SU9721

In about 1688 the 6th Duke of
Somerset rebuilt the medieval home
of the Percy's, creating an edifice as
imposing as any great French
château. To complete it the Duke's
descendant, the 2nd Earl of
Egremont, had a deer park and
pleasure grounds landscaped in
1752 by Capability Brown on an
equally grand scale. Petworth
remained in the same family until in
1947 house and grounds were given
to the National Trust.

The Carved Room boasts
incredible work by Grinling
Gibbons and estate workman John
Selden. Also most impressive is the
Grand Staircase, with painted walls
and ceiling in the baroque manner.

Petworth is a veritable treasury of
paintings, including many oils by
Turner, several Van Dycks and one
painting unmistakably in the style of
Hieronymus Bosch. A collection of
sculptures is housed in a gallery
which was specially built for it.

The small town of Petworth is
compact, seeming to be pressed up
against the overshadowing high
walls of Petworth House. Its
mellow houses echo its long history,
right up to some splendid 16th- and
17th-century residences.

AA recommends:
Guesthouse: Almshouses, Tillington, *tel.*
(0798) 43432
Garages: Heath End (Rapley & Son), *tel.*
(0798) 42461
Driveflash Ltd, Hampers Common, *tel.*
(0798) 43541
Harwoods Ltd, North End, *tel.* (0798)
42232

*The Long Gallery at Parham, 158ft
long by 18ft wide, is a treasury of fine
furniture and various objets d'art*

Left: impression of Roman Anderida, remains of which survive at Pevensey

Pevensey Castle was built inside the Roman wall of Anderida around 1080, 14 years after William I landed near by

Pevensey

Map Ref: 87TQ6404

The Romans built the fort of *Anderida* here in about AD300, and their sturdy 12ft-thick outer walls remain today. In 1066 William the Conqueror landed at Pevensey, which in those days was an important seaport, and left his half brother Robert there while he went on to defeat Harold – the last Saxon king of England – at the Battle of Hastings. Robert built a moated castle in a corner of the 10-acre fort, with a stone keep and walls of earth that were replaced in the 13th century by a curtain wall with gatehouse and three towers.

Although besieged four times during its long history and twice starved into surrender, the castle was never taken by force. It was re-armed in Elizabethan times against the Armada, and prepared for defence again during World War II when Canadians (in 1942) and Americans (in 1943) were billeted there. Ancient fireplaces, dungeons and an oubliette where prisoners were put and forgotten about can still be seen.

Up the lane from the castle is a 13th-century church with some interesting items on display, including a Norman stone pestle for pounding grain; a box of 1703 with an inkwell, sprinkler for drying the ink, and candle holder for the wax; Crusaders' tombstones; and a great parish chest dated 1664.

Pevensey's days as a sea port were over in 1714, when its harbour silted up, but its past prosperity can be gauged by the fact that in Norman times it minted its own coins. Today there is a 14th-century Mint House on the site. Also in the village street of cobbled and flint cottages is The Court House and Gaol building, which became the smallest Town Hall in the country until Pevensey Corporation was dissolved in 1886. Today it houses a museum with exhibits including: a rare coat of arms of William and Mary; a collection of Victoriana; old photographs; ironware and blacksmiths' tools. The cells below can also be seen.

AA recommends:
Hotel: Priory Court Inn, Castle Rd, 2-star, *tel.* (0323) 763150
Guesthouse: Napier, The Promenade, Pevensey Bay, *tel.* (0323) 768875

Piddinghoe

Map Ref: 87TQ4303

An old rhyme that goes:
> *Englishmen fight and Frenchmen too.*
> *We don't, we live in Piddinghoe*
is probably remembered today just to show how the name of the village is pronounced. The village lies on a wide curve of the River Ouse about a mile north of Newhaven, and was once a popular place for smugglers and a stop for sailing barges when iron was an important trade. Today, small boats belonging to deep-sea anglers and week-end sailors are moored on the quayside just below the church, one of only three in Sussex to have a round Norman tower.

Inside is a modern stained-glass window, donated in 1983 to the memory of Dr Elizabeth Holmes, who lived in the village. Another older memorial gives pleasure to local children today. When little Edith Croft died in 1868 at 13 weeks old, her mother provided a fund in her memory. Known as Little Edith's Treat, it still provides a treat for village children.

All three round-towered churches in Sussex are strung out along the River Ouse, and may have served as beacons

Glyndebourne

Before his marriage in 1931 to the accomplished opera singer Audrey Mildmay, John Christie had been a regular visitor to the major European music festivals and was determined to built a small, intimate theatre at Glyndebourne in order to entertain friends. His wife persuaded him to 'do the thing properly', and the result was a theatre capable of accommodating 300 with a good-sized orchestra pit and excellent stage facilities. Glyndebourne opened on 28 May 1934, with a performance of Mozart's *Marriage of Figaro*. The venture was hardly an instant success; only seven souls in evening dress boarded the train from Victoria on the second day!

But the Christies persevered, helped by several factors – not least being that the building of Glyndebourne coincided with the rise of the Nazis in Germany. Two of the many artists who declined to collaborate with the Nazis were Fritz Busch and Carl Ebert, respectively conductor at Dresden and director and producer of the Berlin State Opera. Both men had established world-wide reputations and their availability, and readiness to help with the launching of this new venture, was undoubtedly an enormous bonus for Glyndebourne.

Audrey Mildmay's initial insistence on concentrating on the repertoire of Mozart's operas was another advantage – she instinctively felt that this most elegant of music suited Glyndebourne better than her husband's original choice of Wagner. By 1939, the theatre had been enlarged to seat 600; it now accommodates 830.

With the exception of the war

Guests enjoying the gardens at the start of the Festival in June 1954

years and from 1948–9, when Glyndebourne staged productions at the Edinburgh Festival, Glyndebourne has continued to present opera in unmatched surroundings to full houses. The repertoire has expanded to include the work of neglected composers like Monteverdi, and modern classics such as Britten's *Rape of Lucretia* and *Albert Herring*.

The many outstanding artists from all over the world who have appeared there indicate the importance which the operatic world attaches to this most remarkable of opera houses.

Preparation for the role of Ilia in a production of Mozart's Idomeneo

Reminder of perhaps the biggest hoax suffered by the archaeological world

Piltdown

Map Ref: 87TQ4422

In December 1912 Charles Dawson, a Lewes solicitor and amateur geologist, told the Geological Society that he had found fragments of a skull that could be the missing link in Man's development half a million years ago. This exciting anouncement put the tiny hamlet of Piltdown, between Haywards Heath and Uckfield, firmly on the map. The skull was placed in the British Museum, and the local pub changed its name from The Lamb to The Piltdown Man.

However, today people come to the place where it was found in the grounds of Barcombe Manor – the spot marked with a memorial stone erected in 1938 – more out of curiosity than pilgrimage. For in the 1950s tests showed that the whole thing was a gigantic hoax that had

fooled the archaeological world. Piltdown Man, as it had become known, had never existed. No one knows for sure if the hoax was perpetrated by Dawson, or if he himself had been used as a tool by the hoaxers.

Nearby Piltdown Pond is popular with anglers and for picnics, and around it is a golf course that is said to have been the site of a plague pit for victims of the Black Death.

Plumpton

Map Ref: 86TQ3513

This is a divided village. Plumpton Green and its modern houses adjoin the railway station, with its National Hunt racecourse to the south. The older part is two miles away and has the 16th-century moated Plumpton Place (not open to the public), a post office, a pub, and a flint-built church with nave walls dating from the 12th century. This is reached, since East Sussex Agricultural College was built, along a narrow track past greenhouses on one side, and chicken coups on the other. Traffic rumbles along the road between it and the Downs, but inside (the key can be obtained from the Agricultural College) are 12th-century wall paintings that were uncovered in 1956.

Up a footpath opposite the college is the site of an Early Bronze Age settlement, and near by a sandstone block commemorates the Battle of Lewes, fought in 1264, when Simon de Montfort defeated Henry III.

AA recommends:
Campsites: Gallops Farm, Streat La, Streat, Hassocks, Venture Site, *tel.* (0273) 890387, (1¾ m NW)
Plumpton Racecourse (TRAX), Caravan · Club Site, Plumpton Green, 2-pennants, *tel.* (0273) 890522

The flint fabric of Pyecombe's ancient church is typical of vernacular architecture on the chalk downland

Restaurant: Stane Street Hollow, Codmore Hill, 1-fork, 1-rosette, *tel.* (07982) 2819
Garage: Harwoods, London Rd, *tel.* (07982) 2407

Pyecombe

Map Ref: 86TQ2912

This small village, situated on either side of the A23 at its junction with the A281, was once known for making the best shepherd's crooks obtainable. The curled end of the crook, called the guide, is distinctive on a Pyecombe, and more efficient for catching sheep – though difficult to make. Sometimes it was fashioned from an old gun barrel. Throughout the 1800s and well into the 1900s a Mr Berry and later a Mr Mitchell forged the world-famous crooks, which – sadly – are no longer made there. Several rare old Pyecombe crooks can be seen in Worthing Museum.

Pyecombe's connection with the crook is shown on the village signs, and a crook is included in the design of the church gateway. In the church there is a 12th-century drum-shaped lead font, one of three still in Sussex. The church also boasts one of seven surviving tapsell gates, which are unique to Downs' churches. These pivot on a central pin, and their origin is unknown.

Ringmer

Map Ref: 87TQ4412

One of the earliest settlements recorded in the history of Sussex is Ringmer, which stands three miles north-east of Lewes on the road to Heathfield, and has a wide green fringed with cottages. A place of worship has stood on the site occupied by the 14th-century church for over 1,000 years, but nothing remains of the Norman building that replaced the Saxon one except the bases of the pillars in the nave, and some stones in the south wall carved with Norman ornaments. The tower has been burnt down twice, in the 16th and early 19th centuries, and the present one was built in 1884 by William Martin – who is said to have made the first wooden-wheeled cycle in England!

It was in Ringmer too that Timothy Tortoise, made famous by naturalist Gilbert White, lived with White's aunt at Delves House. The tortoise's picture is on the signpost leading to the church, and his shell is in the Natural History Museum.

On the parish boundary of Ringmer and Glynde is Glyndebourne (see panel), John Christie's gift to opera in the south.

WELL & PUMP
CONSTRUCTED & PRESENTED
TO THE
PARISH OF RINGMER
FOR THE USE OF THE
INHABITANTS & WAYFARERS
BY
R. & S. H. RICKMAN.
1873

Pulborough

Map Ref: 85TQ0418

Built on the course of the Roman Stane Street and close to the River Arun – which here is spanned by several old bridges – this village retains a pleasant atmosphere despite being at the crossing of two major roads, the A29 and A283. In the main part of the village, which runs along the river, can be seen attractive stone and half-timbered houses. The large church stands a little apart with a cluster of

Drawing well water became easier for the residents of Ringmer when this public pump was presented to the parish during the 19th century

Georgian houses on high ground to the north, and is considered an excellent example of the Perpendicular style. Particularly noteworthy are a 12th-century font and an impressive brass dating from the 15th century.

AA recommends:
Hotel: Chequers, Church Pl, 1-star, *tel.* (07982) 2486

Rodmell

Map Ref: 87TQ4105

About half-way between Lewes and Newhaven off the A275, this little village of flint walls and thatched cottages is said to have got its name from the 'mill on the road'. No mill exists there today, but Mill Road commemorates its former existence and in the little 12th-century church is an old picture with the name of the village spelt 'Rodmill'. The church is reached, rather strangely, through a school playground.

Rodmell's main claim to fame is that it was the home for many years of novelist Virginia Woolf, who lived in Monk's House (see page 57), which now belongs to the National Trust, and is open twice a week in summer months. Only 15 people are allowed in at a time, so it is wise to telephone first. The village may not have a miller – but it does have father-and-son blacksmiths, working from a building that has been dated 1850. Actually this is the date of the building's conversion and it has in fact been a workshop for almost 200 years.

A mile or so up the road is Breaky Bottom, one of the most beautifully situated vineyards in England. It is reached by a chalky path leading up on to the Downs and covers about six acres. Customers can try different wines in an ancient farm courtyard before deciding which to buy – and may enjoy strains of opera drifting from the house. Owner Peter Hall is an opera enthusiast, and it was in the great barn here that the New Sussex Opera was born.

Forging at Rodmell's smithy

scented gardens, rare plants and ramped paths that make it suitable for wheelchairs.

Sir Edward Burne Jones – his wife was Kipling's aunt and Prime Minister Stanley Baldwin was his nephew – lived from 1880 to 1898 at North End House, now divided into three. He designed, and William Morris made, seven windows in the church across the green. Artist Sir William Nicholson lived just before World War I in the 250-year-old Grange, now the local library, which has a Kipling memorial room, art gallery, Sussex room and a selection from Brighton Museum's toy collection. Another resident was a German bank clerk named J Reuter, who started a pigeon post to bring news from abroad – the beginning of the now world-wide news agency.

AA recommends:
Guesthouses: Braemar House, Steyning Rd, *tel.* (0273) 34263
Corner House, Steyning Rd, *tel.* (0273) 34533

Seaford

Map Ref: 87TV4899

Before the River Ouse changed course to Newhaven in the 16th century, Seaford was an important port. Today little remains of the old town except the church, and people come for its good shops and three-mile-long promenade overlooking a shingly beach. From the top of Seaford Head are magnificent views of the white cliffs of the Seven Sisters, and a nature reserve covers 308 acres of mudflat, meadowland and downland between the Cuckmere River and the headland. Some 250 species of plants can be found, there are ducks and waders, fossils can be seen in the cliffs and rock pools hold sea anemones. Also, the chalk slopes support a rich flora.

The Martello Tower at the eastern end of the Esplanade is the most westerly in a chain of 103 similar fortresses built on the coast from Aldeburgh to Seaford as a first line of defence against Napoleon. Today the Seaford tower houses a Museum of Local History, containing an extraordinary variety of items such as a gun platform, a wartime kitchen, a working model railway, 'Old Tyme' shops and historical records and photos.

AA recommends:
Guesthouse: Avondale Hotel, 5 Avondale Rd, *tel.* (0323) 890008

Bygone grocery packaging displayed in Seaford's Napoleonic Martello tower as the shelf stock of an old-time shop

Dolls from the National Toy Museum displayed at Rottingdean's Grange Museum and Art Gallery, which is in a Georgian house remodelled by Lutyens

Rottingdean

Map Ref: 86TQ3602

There must be plenty of plant-lovers in Rottingdean today, for there seem to be flowers everywhere. The Rudyard Kipling Garden (he lived at The Elms from 1897 to 1902) was saved from being built on in 1983 by the local Preservation Society, and is now a delight to wander in. It has old stone walls, a formal rose garden, wild and

Selsey

Map Ref: 84SZ8593

The Saxon King Aethelwach gave land near Selsey for Wilfrid, Bishop of York, to set up his bishopric in AD683. Wilfrid built a chapel and monastery there, which were used until the see was moved to Chichester in 1070, and subsequently both cathedral and monastery disappeared under the waves as victims of severe coastal erosion. In the 13th century a new church was built, which survived until it was divided in 1866 – the nave then being removed and re-erected to make a church in Selsey village. The chancel was blocked off and left on the original site at Church Norton.

Beside it today is Pagham Harbour, which was formed when the sea breached reclaimed land in 1910. A local nature reserve and a well-known refuge for rare birds, it features a planned nature trail and is a favourite resort of ornithologists. Selsey has always suffered from coastal erosion and change. The name derives from Seal's Island, and it really was an island before it became joined to the mainland as the Manhood Peninsula, with Selsey Bill at its tip – today an agglomeration of holiday homes. In the 16th century more erosion took place, and a whole deer park was lost to the waves. Selsey has long been known for its cockles, which were one of the traditional fish dishes of the region – along with Arundel mullet, Chichester lobster and Amberley trout. In the early 19th century the extraordinary Colin Pullinger emerged, claiming dozens of skills and noted in local history as proprietor of a flourishing mousetrap industry. It is said that the quaint Hundred of Manhood and Selsey Tramway was built primarily to transport the mousetraps to Chichester, for

world-wide distribution – though in its day it also carried 80,000 passengers a year.

Sheffield Park

Map Ref: 87TQ4124

Sheffield Park is neither a hamlet nor a village, but it does have a stately home and beautiful gardens (see page 29), a steam railway and a large pub – all on the A275 between Lewes and East Grinstead. Sheffield Park house was built in the 18th century for the 1st Earl of Sheffield in a Tudor style that was later remodelled as Gothic, and stands in gardens laid out by Lancelot 'Capability' Brown. It was in the library here that Gibbon wrote much of his epic *Decline and Fall of the Roman Empire*, and he is buried in Fletching chuch at the other end of the park. The 3rd Earl, a cricketing enthusiast, organised the first tours of Australian cricket teams in England, and the introductory matches were always played at Sheffield Park.

The 3rd Lord Sheffield would probably have been pleased at the success today of the Bluebell

Between May and June the gardens of Sheffield Park are ablaze with a huge variety of azaleas and rhododendrons

Working boats at isolated Selsey Bill

Railway. He was in the chair when the Lewes and East Grinstead Railway Company was first formed in 1876, and would not have approved of the Beeching cuts that closed it in the 1950s. A few years later, a group of steam-train enthusiasts got together to form the Bluebell Railway Preservation Society, and today the trains puff through the bluebell woods between Horsted Keynes and Sheffield Park. Part of a station on the revived line houses a museum of railway relics.

Just up the road is the 18th-century Sheffield Arms, a stopping place for travellers for 200 years. It was built in 1777 by John Holroyd, the 1st Earl of Sheffield, and his initials can be seen on a stone at the back. It is said that a cave behind it was used as a store for contraband, and had an underground passage to a farmhouse. About 50 years ago it was decided to test the story. Three ducks were shut in the cave and 10 days later one re-appeared in the farmhouse cellar!

Steam trains once again work a revived section of the Bluebell Line between Sheffield Park and Horsted Keynes

Downland Windmills

Windmills have been used in this country for centuries, and were commonplace in and around the South Downs area until the unpredictable energy of the wind gave way to the certain and consistent power of steam. They quickly declined, eventually becoming derelict landscape features sufficiently rare to excite comment.

Fortunately, some – such as Shipley King's Mill; Jack and Jill at Clayton; Halnaker and Chailey – were rescued before they succumbed completely, and have been restored. Some are even in working order, and grind local grain on a small-scale commercial basis.

Three distinct types of mill can be recognised, known respectively as post, tower and smock. The earliest are post-mills, so called because they were built on a single vertical post around which the whole angular wooden structure could be revolved to face the prevailing wind. It was later realised that there was no need for the whole building to rotate, and tower-mills came into fashion – usually round and built of brick or stone, with rotating caps to which the sails were fixed.

Smock-mills are the most recent and incorporate the rotating cap of the tower-mill with the wooden construction of the post-mill. They acquired their name from the similarity between the shape of the fixed timber frame – usually clad with weather-board – and a farmworker's smock. In Europe they are known as Dutch mills.

Mill sails, known as sweeps in Sussex, were used to send messages. If, for instance, a journeyman stone dresser was needed, the sails would be left just short of the vertical. Set in the square St George's Cross position they were a mark of mourning – and who knows what configurations were used to communicate with the local smuggling gangs, who often hid their contraband in mills.

Good examples of all three types can be seen in the South Downs area: both Shipley King's Mill and Chailey Mill are smocks, with the former being particularly noted for its size; Clayton's 'Jill' is an early post-mill, pre-dated by an even earlier one at Halnaker; and 'Jack' – also at Clayton – is a tower-mill.

Above: a tower-mill (left) and a post-mill with its cross section. Canvas was fixed to the sails' framework and the rigging changed with the wind's strength

Right: writer Hilaire Belloc found it a struggle to keep Shipley Mill in repair, but now it is looked after by a trust fund formed in his memory

Shipley

Map Ref: 85TQ1421

Built in 1879, Shipley King's Mill is one of the few remaining smock-mills in Sussex – and the largest (see panel). In 1906 the poet and writer Hilaire Belloc bought it, along with the nearby house of King's Land. He was often seen to raise his hat to the mill, which was locally known as Mrs Shipley, and after his death in 1953 it was restored to full working order by his friends and local people, as a memorial. After financial support for many years from the West Sussex County Council, in 1986 the mill became funded by a charitable trust.

Hilaire Belloc is not Shipley's only connection with the arts. Wilfrid Scawen Blunt, the poet and traveller, lived there and entertained such guests as Oscar Wilde, William Morris and Winston Churchill. The composer John Ireland is buried in Shipley's churchyard.

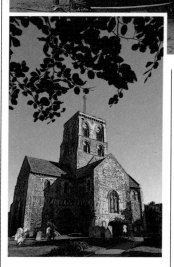

Shoreham stands at the mouth of the Adur and in Norman times became a strategic port serving the important castle town of Bramber. During this period the Church of St May de Haura was built

Shoreham-by-Sea

Map Ref: 86TQ2105

Old Shoreham was a coastal town founded by AElla the Saxon, but when in the late Middle Ages the sea receded the port of New Shoreham was developed and the old town reverted to a village. Now joined by a corridor of buildings, New and Old Shoreham are known collectively as Shoreham-by-Sea.

New Shoreham's notable Norman Church of St Mary de Haura (de Havre) is well worth seeing, and one of the 18th-century houses near its churchyard was the home of Captain Harry Roberts – who sailed with Captain Cook. Another notable citizen was 17th-century mathematician John Pell, whose main claim to fame was that he invented the division sign! Royal connections include one with Charles II, who sailed to France from Shoreham in Captain Tattersall's *Enterprise*. Between Shoreham and Portslade lies Kingston Buci (Kingston-on-Sea, Southwick), which is said to have been named after King Harold. Once a centre for oyster fishing, it is now a quiet little place comprising the 13th-century church of St Julian, a few cottages, a Victorian stone lighthouse and an RNLI lifeboat station.

Across the harbour is the bungalow town of Shoreham Beach, which was destroyed in World War II to prevent it being used as a beach-head, and rebuilt since 1950. Its wooden footbridge is intact, and motorists can reach it from the coast road over the Norfolk Bridge.

Old cottages line Shoreham's narrow streets from the church to the High Street, which runs parallel to the harbour. Here, old and new jostle, and mere yards from Woolworth is one of the oldest secular buildings in England – the Marlipins. Most distinctive with its chequerboard pattern of flint and Caen stone, it now accommodates the town museum. Opposite, the massive figurehead of a pirate juts out from an inn.

AA recommends:
Guesthouse: Pende-Shore Hotel, 416 Upper Shoreham Rd, *tel.* (07917) 2905
Garages: Frosts, 69-75 Brighton Rd, *tel.* (07917) 61411
Keen & Betts, Brighton Rd, *tel.* (07917) 61333
Recovery Services, Dolphin Rd, *tel.* (07917) 27332

Singleton

Map Ref: 84SU8713

Singleton shares the beautiful and secluded valley of the River Lavant, overlooked by Goodwood from high on the Downs, with two other interesting little villages. East Dean has a restored medieval church and neat flint and half-timbered cottages around a willow-hung pond.

Charlton was once the home of the famous Charlton Hunt, the first regular foxhunt in England and a reason for the 1st Duke of Richmond's choice of nearby Goodwood House as his residence. Later moved to Goodwood, in its 18th-century heyday the ancient hunt counted the 2nd Duke of Richmond as its Master. He built Charlton's Fox Hall as a hunting box and at the same time the name of the local inn was changed from The Pig and Whistle to The Fox. In 1985 it became a free house and

was renamed The Fox Goes Free.

Singleton is known today for the Weald and Downland Open Air Museum (see page 69) and Chilsdown Vineyard. England's first Women's Institute was formed there in 1915.

AA recommends:
Garage: Pearmans, Childown, *tel.* (024363) 229

Slindon

Map Ref: 85SU9608

Slindon, just off the busy A29, is a brick-and-flint village which enjoys an enviable situation on wooded downland slopes commanding fine views to the sea. Most of the cottages date from the 17th century, and the Parish Church of St Mary contains a rare 16th-century wooden effigy.

Slindon House, now a boarding school, preserves many Elizabethan features and a few traces of 13th-century work. It was a Catholic headquarters following the Reformation – when even the great castle at Arundel was lying in ruins – and preserves a priest's hiding hole. The other village church, dedicated to St Richard, is of the Roman Catholic faith.

The National Trust's Slindon Estate comprises 3,505 acres of farm and woodland stretching to the northern foot of the South Downs, including Bignor Hill, Cold Harbour Hill and Glatting Beacon. As well as superb beech woods and a variety of other good wildlife habitats, the estate features numerous prehistoric monuments; perhaps the most impressive is the Neolithic causewayed camp of Barkhale.

More recent round barrows exist there too, and one of two ancient crossridge dykes has been breached by the Roman Stane Street – of which a 3½-mile stretch survives on the estate. The sea once penetrated inland this far, and when it retreated it left its shingle beach stranded 130ft above sea level. This can be seen at the western end of the estate.

Sompting

Map Ref: 86TQ1705

A narrow turning north from the A27, opposite the southern turn-off to the village of Sompting, leads to Sompting church (see page 51), which stands high up just a few yards from the main road and is the village's pride and joy. St Mary's has been described as 'the greatest architectural curiosity in England'. It is the only church in the country having a Saxon tower with a Rhenish helm, so-called because many Rhenish Romanesque towers are equipped with it. The church was built about AD1000 and features in *Domesday*. In 1184 it passed to the Knights Templar and after their suppression in 1306, to the Knights Hospitallers – both of whom partially rebuilt it.

Late Bronze Age and Iron Age settlements existed in this area, and in 1971 finds were made of rare pottery, jewellery and a bronze urn, now in Worthing Museum. 'Somp' in the name of Sompting meant marshy ground, but the village is today practically part of the Worthing conurbation. It was known in particular for two of its inhabitants: George Brown, the fastest bowler of his time, who played for Sussex from 1825 to 1841; and author, Edward John Trelawney, a friend of Shelley and Byron.

This fine, 15th-century timber-framed cottage in Mouse Lane served as Steyning's workhouse at one time

THE LATE MR. E. J. TRELAWNY.

Author Edward Trelawny, who lived in Sompting, involved himself in Lord Byron's romantic but abortive campaign for an independent Greece

which is in the British Museum. In 1604, when a widower in the parish remarried, a humorous rector made the entry in the Register and added in Latin: 'A shipwrecked sailor seeks a second shipwreck.'

Steyning

Map Ref: 86TQ1711

This attractive and ancient little market town has a High Street that closely follows the line of the Downs hidden behind it. Behind the car park, or through a narrow 'twitten' farther down the street, are the Memorial Playing Fields, where cricket is played against the gently curving backdrop of Steyning Round Hill. Sweeping views of woods and sloping fields extend from here to Chanctonbury Ring, in the west (see page 39).

The story of Steyning (pronounced Stenning) began with 8th-century St Cuthman, an early Celtic Christian who travelled from Wessex pushing his invalid mother in a wheeled handcart. On reaching Saxon Steyning, the rope which held the wheel broke and St Cuthman took this as a sign from God to settle there.

The present church of St Andrew stands near the site. It was built in the 12th century by the Normandy Abbey of Fecamp – to which the manor of Steyning and its church had been given by Edward the Confessor. This Norman church is magnificent. The lofty nave, Romanesque arches and massive columns with richly carved capitals are

Southease

Map Ref: 87TQ4205

There was a thriving community at Southease when *Domesday* was written in 1086, but its history goes even farther back – to 966, when the Anglo-Saxon King Edgar issued a charter granting the church and manor to Hyde Abbey in Winchester. A tiny village in a dip of the Lewes–Newhaven road, between Rodmell and Piddinghoe, it has an ancient church that stands by the green and has one of Sussex's three round Norman towers. Inside are patches of 13th-century wall paintings, discovered in the 1930s. The unusual organ has a mahogany case and gilt pipes and was built in 1790 by Allen of Soho. The only others of its kind believed to be still in existence are in Buckingham Palace, St Mary's, Westminster and York Minster. On the wall is a copy of King Edgar's charter, the original of outstanding. The south doors still have their original sanctuary rings on the outside, offering safety to any fugitive who clung to them.

Steyning history can be read in its rich variety of vernacular buildings. The town centre is designated an Outstanding Conservation Area, with 61 buildings of architectural or historical interest. In Church Street is the thatched Saxon Cottage, with its roof steeply pitched in a catslide. Near by is Chantry Green, scene of the martyrdom of Protestant John Launder, who was burned slowly at the stake in 1555. Opposite the High Street car park a clock tower and belfry surmount a small, 17th-century building on which a painted sign announces:

George Fox, Founder of the Society of Friends (The Quakers) held a meeting here in 1655.

There is an excellent little museum in the town, showing local history and prehistoric finds, and a number of 'Horsham-slab' roofs.

AA recommends:
Guesthouses: Down House, King's Barn Villas, *tel.* (0903) 812319
Nash Hotel, Horsham Rd, *tel.* (0903) 814988
Self Catering: Down House Flats, King's Barn Villas, *tel.* (0903) 812319
Nash, Horsham Rd (cottage & flats), *tel.* (0903) 814988

Medieval wall paintings and a rare Norman round tower are features of Southease church, a Saxon foundation dating from at least AD966

Christian fish symbolism and the dove of peace are two of many embroidered hassock designs produced by the congregation of Sullington church

Storrington

Map Ref: 85TQ0814

The village of Storrington has a place in literature, for Francis Thompson was inspired by its surrounding countryside to produce his poem, *Daisy*, which was written while he was staying in a local monastery. Arnold Bax, the composer, lived in the local hostelry from 1940 to 1952.

At the end of the 19th century part of the churchyard was known as the Old Pillery Gardens. This was not a misspelling of pillory, but referred to the occupation of a Mr Dixon – who made and sold pills. His house was dubbed the Pill Factory by local people, and later shortened to Pillery.

Half a mile east of Storrington along the A283 is a narrow turning towards the Downs, signposted 'Sullington Church'. This lane quite unexpectedly ends in the middle of a farm where – elevated on a grassy bank and almost hidden by giant yews – stands the little Saxon Church of St Mary.

The interior is simple and beautiful. In an alcove just inside the entrance, resting on a Saxon stone coffin, lies the marble effigy of a knight. He might have been a Crusader but cannot be dated more accurately than 12th to 14th century. Dr A J Cronin, who bought the old rectory and glebelands down the lane in the 1930s, was inspired by it to write his book *The Crusaders. The Citadel* was also written there.

The knight was probably a member of the de Couvert family, lords of the manor who had come over with William the Conqueror. The effigy was defaced and damaged during the Reformation. Sullington church is not alone in possessing hassocks sewn by its parishioners, but these deserve special mention. Since 1960 its small congregation has designed and embroidered a quite magnificent collection.

The old manor house behind the church is a fine example of Saxon open-hall construction. In its garden peacocks strut, but just yards away are the cowsheds – for it is also a working farm, renowned for its great medieval tithe barn. The date 1685 carved on one of its beams is probably when it was restored. It is 115ft long, as lofty as a church and with not a nail used anywhere in its precise construction. It is remarkable that both church and manor house are in use today as they were nearly 1,000 years ago.

Sullington Warren, which is reached by a side road off the A283 opposite the lane to the church, is a National Trust estate of 30 acres, with views of the Downs.

AA recommends:
Restaurants: Manleys, Manleys Hill, 3-fork, 1-rosette, *tel.* (09066) 2331
Cottage Tandoori, 25 West St, 1-fork, *tel.* (09066) 3605

Sullington, *see* Storrington

Telscombe

Map Ref: 87TQ4003

Just past Rodmell on the A26 Lewes–Newhaven road a turning to the right rises high on to the Downs, giving a stupendous view of the combe below. After two miles the road swoops down to the village of Telscombe, with a Saxon church that can have changed little over the centuries. The list of rectors dates from 1337, and the two Mass dials which can be seen on the corner of the capped tower were once used to tell villagers when it was time for a service.

Along the quiet lane is the 16th-century Manor House, where smugglers once stored their goods. Given to the National Trust in 1960, this is now a lodging place for visiting judges. There is an old rectory too, and a village school where the teacher lived on the premises and taught all the children in one room. The stables at Stud House were once occupied by racehorses, and in 1902 one of them – Shannon Lass – won the Grand National. Its owner, Ambrose Gorham, was so delighted that he celebrated by restoring the church, and each Christmas gave every child a book and a pair of Wellington boots.

Sheep once grazed on the hills above the village and there is a footpath to Telscombe Cliff, now a suburb of Peacehaven.

Uppark

Map Ref: 84SU7717

The red-brick house of Uppark was built for the 1st Earl of Tankerville in about 1690, high on the South Downs, with far vistas towards the sea. In 1747 it was bought by Matthew Fetherstonhaugh, who came to live there with a vast fortune and a charming young wife, Sarah Lethieullier. They made great changes in the house and added a fabulous collection of furniture, carpets and works of art. A favourite feature among visitors is the dolls' house and its exquisite miniature contents, which were made for Sarah Lethieullier. Sir Matthew and Sarah also changed the outside of the house, to almost the form in which it is seen today.

Sir Matthew was succeeded in 1774 by his son Harry. Six years later, Sir Harry brought Emma Hart to Uppark. She was 15 years old, an ignorant country girl of great beauty. After a year or so he tired of her and sent her away with hardly a penny. Emma, however, was not left in that situation for long. As the National Trust guidebook so succinctly puts it: 'Greville befriended her; Romney painted her; Sir William Hamilton married her; and Nelson loved her.'

Sir Harry showed impeccable taste in the additions he found time to make to his parent's collection between bouts of hunting, racing, gambling and entertaining on a grand scale. Eventually he quarrelled with the Prince Regent, a frequent

Rolling downland above the Ouse Valley, near Telscombe Farm

visitor, and after 1810 retired from society – having engaged Repton to add the north portico.

In 1825, when he was over 70, Sir Harry married young Mary Ann Bullock, his head dairymaid. After his death in 1846 the erstwhile dairymaid and her unmarried sister Frances were at pains to keep the house 'as Sir 'arry 'ad it' until Frances's death in 1895. This meant that the 18th- and early 19th-century interior escaped Victorian restoration. Uppark's romantic history was enhanced when in 1880 a Mrs Wells – mother of author H G Wells – became the housekeeper.

To their great credit, the owners of the house in this century have carefully fostered the preservation made by Mary Ann and Frances, and the National Trust – to whom Uppark was given in 1954 – continues to protect and conserve.

Within the superb neo-classical shell of Uppark, which stands in 54-acre grounds, is a remarkably complete and unspoiled 18th-century interior

Weald and Downland Open Air Museum

Map Ref: 84SU8613

On a 40-acre site in the beautiful Lavant Valley, this famous museum has a unique collection of 30 historic buildings that were rescued from their original sites when threatened with destruction. The variety is astonishing and ranges from medieval times to the 19th century, including: a Wealden house; a 19th-century village school; a treadwheel; a toll cottage; buildings grouped round a market hall; and others in woodland. Many more are in store, awaiting re-erection.

Rural crafts pursued at the museum include: corn grinding in the water-mill (the flour is sold at the museum shop); thatching-spar production, using timber from a coppiced wood near by; and there is a charcoal burner's camp in the woods. For centuries charcoal burning was a major industry in the Weald for fuelling the iron industry (see page 71), and has existed within living memory.

Generations of burners lived with their families in small turf huts in the forest next to their kilns, which had to be watched day and night. At the museum a more modern iron kiln is used, which is loaded and lit twice a week; the charcoal is sold for barbecues. Special demonstrations in season include carpentry and blacksmithing, lead working, sheep-dog trials, heavy-horse ploughing, sheep shearing and spinning. Considerable attention is paid to keeping children interested, and an introductory exhibition gives both general and particular information about the museum.

West Burton

Map Ref: 85TQ0014

Signposted from the A285 south of Duncton, the working water-mill at Burton was built in 1780 on the site of an old forge that had been used by the Wealden iron industry, which flourished in the 16th and 17th centuries (see page 71). By the end of the 17th century charcoal burning and the use of timber for shipbuilding had destroyed large tracts of Wealden forest, and iron smelting was forced to move to the coal-rich north.

Burton mill produced flour from

The central hall and hearth of 15th-century Bayleaf Farmhouse, at the Weald and Downland Museum

around 1780 until the early 1900s, when it fell into disuse, then in 1960 West Sussex County Council acquired both the mill and the pond and repaired the dam which stood between them. The pond is now a nature reserve surrounded by a nature trail, and has a rich variety of flora and fauna.

In 1978 the County Council decided to lease the mill for flour production, on condition that the tenant repaired it. A young man appropriately named William Mills accepted the challenge and set about restoring the derelict and almost gutted old building. An unusual feature to have survived was a water turbine used instead of the traditional water-wheel; it is thought to be the only one in the county. Extensive repairs were carried out by volunteers, and a pair of French Burr millstones were brought from a disused mill. Charles Muddle, who came from an old Sussex milling family, repaired the millstones and their equipment with the help of many volunteers. By 1980 the mill was ready for the stones to be dressed.

Westdean

Map Ref: 87TV5299

This secluded little East Sussex village in the heart of Friston Forest, just six miles west of Eastbourne, can be reached on foot 'over the hill and through the woods', or by a little lane off the A259 from Cuckmere Haven. It is believed to be the town known as Dene, where Alfred the Great kept a fleet, for in Saxon times the Cuckmere formed a wider and deeper estuary. It is also thought that his palace stood where now lie the ruins of a medieval manor, with a circular flint dovecote almost hidden behind high flint walls.

From Westdean a section of the South Downs Way path leads to Litlington, and in the adjacent woodlands are 2¾-mile and circular forest walks. Half a mile to the north is Charleston Manor, recorded in *Domesday*, under the name of Cerlestone, as belonging to William the Conqueror's cup bearer.

West Dean

Map Ref: 84SU8612

A charity trust set up by the unconventional Edward James in 1964 transformed his home, West Dean House, into a college of arts and crafts. He himself, married to dancer Tilly Losch, was a collector and patron of surrealist art, and a friend of surrealist painter Salvador Dali.

The College is not open to garden visitors, but the exterior is worth a close look. Designed by James Wyatt in 1804, the house is built entirely of flints and shows remarkable galleting – in which the mortar between the flints is studded with tiny slivers of flint, with their sharp edges protruding. This painstaking work is said to have been by French prisoners taken during the Napoleonic Wars. The layout of the gardens today has changed little since 1804, when they were redesigned (see page 28).

A grant from the Sussex Historic Gardens Restoration Society has allowed the renovation of a Victorian summerhouse; in addition, the grounds feature a gazebo, a 350ft-long pergola, a walled kitchen garden restored to its Edwardian splendour – and an interesting collection of early tools and lawn mowers.

West Hoathly

Map Ref: 85TQ3632

High on a hill, this pretty village has tile-hung and weather-boarded cottages surrounding an ancient church. From its 15th-century tower there is a panoramic view (on

a clear day) over to the South Downs from Beachy Head to the Ouse.

Almost opposite the church is the 500-year-old Priest's House, built of timber with wattle and daub filling. In the garden, fanned trees form a backdrop to a wide herbaceous border, and there is a fine topiary hedge. The furniture is mainly of the 18th and 19th centuries, and displays of kitchenware, samplers

West Dean Gardens, where there are summerhouses, a pergola, a walled garden and Victorian glasshouses among the shrubberies and borders

Aylesbury and mallard ducks at the peaceful village pond in Westdean

and needlework can be seen.

Outside the village, but within the parish, is Gravetye Manor – now an hotel, but once the home of a local iron master. Later it was used by smugglers and later still it was the home of William Robinson, a 19th-century gardening correspondent of *The Times*, who created Gravetye's beautiful garden.

West Wittering

Map Ref: 84SZ7898

According to local legend, when the 1st century AD Roman General Vespasian landed somewhere near West Wittering on his way to take Chichester, some of his elephants became stuck in the mud. Today West Wittering is known for its sandy beach, which attracts more tourists than any of the other Chichester Harbour villages.

The village itself stands outside the harbour, behind the sand spit of East Head – an unusual feature that has only survived on this shifting coastline through intensive conservation in recent years. A National Trust Nature Walk of just over a mile explores the beach and sand dunes of which it is composed.

Exiled Bishop Wilfrid of York, who brought Christianity to Sussex, was welcomed by the Saxon King Aethelwalch at nearby Selsey in AD 683. He established a cathedral there and at the Witterings, known then as Withtrynges, which was transferred to Chichester. The area was part of Cakeham Manor, of which the house survives.

Ancient 'wreck rights' belonging to the manor were exploited by local smugglers, who floated their contraband ashore as if it had come from wrecks.

West Wittering was once well

Pilgrims' crosses on the chancel pillar in West Wittering's church

known for its Christmas mummers, called 'Tipteers' in Sussex, comprising half a dozen men or boys who performed a traditional play with words which had been handed down orally from one generation to the next until at least the end of the 19th century.

AA recommends:
Campsite: Wicks Farm Caravan Park, Redlands La, 3-pennants, *tel.* (0243) 513116

The Wealden Iron Industry

From the late Iron Age until the 19th century, Wealden sandstone yielded ore which supported a thriving iron industry in parts of Sussex. A great deal of evidence remains of this, and the period is reflected in names which occur frequently, particularly in the Weald – for instance, Furnace Green, Cinder Hill and Forge Cottage.

The Romans brought to Sussex many skills and crafts, among them iron-working, and Romano–British furnaces have been discovered on the Weald near Crawley, and at Sedlescombe and Westfield near the Kent border. By-products such as slag and cinder were used to metal Roman roads.

From Roman times the industry survived, albeit spasmodically, until in the 15th and 16th centuries the introduction of new techniques from abroad transformed it. The Sussex Weald became a veritable Black Country, full of iron mines.

Hammer ponds provided heads of water to drive bellows for blast furnaces, which extracted crude ore, and trip hammers for beating out the metal. These ponds can still be found throughout the county – one has been landscaped into the gardens at Leonardslee (see page 27), and another forms part of a nature reserve at West Burton (see page 69).

Evidence of the prosperity brought by the industry in Tudor times abounds on the Weald. Rudyard Kipling's home, Bateman's, is a fine example of an ironmaster's house, and many Wealden churches contain the graves of these early industrialists. They lie under embossed cast-iron slabs that bear mute testimony to their craft and carry likenesses of their tools along with tales of their achievements.

By the early 19th century Sussex's source of iron ore had dwindled, and richer veins had been discovered outside the county. The industry declined, but later in the century John Every settled in Lewes and set up an iron foundry. Much of the wrought ironwork – railings and balconies – still to be found in Brighton came from the foundry, which at the height of its success was destroyed by fire. However, Every's reputation was such that clients, friends and neighbours all lent him money to build a new foundry – aptly named the Phoenix Iron Works. An excellent collection of cast-iron firebacks, decorated with the makers' devices and inscriptions, can be seen in Lewes at Anne of Cleves' House.

This fine Sussex fire back is part of a collection kept in timber-framed Anne of Cleves' House, Lewes

Wilmington

Map Ref: 87TQ5404

No one knows who created The Long Man of Wilmington, a giant figure some 227ft tall, cut into the turf of Windover Hill. Guesses as to when it first appeared go back to the Bronze Age, and suggestions as to who it might be include King Harold of the Saxons, a creation of Priory monks, and a Roman soldier.

No one will ever be sure – but what is known is that it was first mentioned in 1779, outlined in yellow bricks in 1873, and given its present outline in 1969 with 700 white concrete blocks.

A good view of it can be enjoyed from the car park of the 11th-century Benedictine Priory, founded in 1050 as an out-station of the Benedictine Abbey of Grestain, in Normandy. Little remains of the Priory today except the crypt, the ruins of the 14th-century Great Hall, parts of the Gate House and the Prior's Chapel. It ceased to be a religious house in 1413, and in later centuries became a farm. Since 1925 it has been run by the Sussex Archaeological Society.

Today it has an enjoyable and immaculately kept agricultural museum (open to the public from mid March to mid October) where can be seen old farming implements and machinery – and kitchen and household utensils including the first domestic tin-opener of 1871, curling irons and bed warmers. In the kitchen, a 16th-century menu hangs over a fireplace which has an iron pot and long-handled salamander.

Worthing

Map Ref: 86TQ1402

In 1798 George III's daughter Princess Amelia came to convalesce at Worthing – then a small fishing village – and contemporary nobility

The remains of Wilmington Priory, incorporated in an 18th-century farmhouse, and the Church of St Mary and St Peter

followed close behind. The resulting spate of building overwhelmed many surrounding villages, leaving only their parish churches and a few old buildings amongst the Regency developments. Broadwater's Norman church is the oldest, and Tarring is known for its 137ft spire, which was used as a look-out station during the Armada threat 400 years ago. The church itself is dedicated to St Andrew and dates from the 12th century. A row of 15th-century close-timbered cottages in Tarring High Street is made up of the oldest inhabited houses in the borough.

Worthing Pier is a Victorian contribution. Over 900ft long, it was opened in 1862 and rebuilt after a storm in 1914. Popular with holidaymakers, it is also favoured by sea anglers and has a Pavilion.

Man has lived in and around Worthing since prehistoric times, and Highdown Hill – behind the town – is an important

Regency terraces and 20th-century light bulbs on Worthing seafront

archaeological site where in 1890 a Saxon cemetery was uncovered. Weapons, glass, pottery and jewellery of the 5th and 6th centuries found there can be seen at Worthing Museum. Also on Highdown Hill is the Gloomy Miller's Tomb. He was John Olliver of Ferring, who kept a coffin under his bed and erected his tomb 25 years before he needed it, in 1791. More cheerfully, the hill is a good viewpoint.

Worthing today is the largest seaside resort in West Sussex, and has all the usual trappings. They include a symphony orchestra, and music from classical to 'rock and pop' is a feature of the town. It has also become the home of bowls championships, and the Connaught Theatre was reopened in 1987 as a centre for theatre, films, ballet, opera and all kinds of related activity.

AA recommends:
Hotels: Beach, Marine Pde, 3-star, *tel.* (0903) 34001
Chatsworth, The Steyne, 3-star, *tel.* (0903) 36103
Beechwood Hall, Richmond Rd, 2-star, *tel.* (0903) 32872
Kingsway, Marine Pde, 2-star, *tel.* (0903) 37542
Restaurant: Paragon Continental, 9-10 Brunswick Rd, 2-fork, *tel.* (0903) 33367
Guesthouses: Meldrum House, 8 Windsor Rd, *tel.* (0903) 33808
Moorings Private Hotel, 4 Selden Rd, *tel.* (0903) 208882
Wansfell Hotel, 49 Chesswood Rd, *tel.* (0903) 30612
Windsor House Hotel, 14-20 Windsor Rd, *tel.* (0903) 39655
Self Catering: Chesswood, 56 Homefield Rd (flats), *tel.* (0903) 38512
Hill Top, Mill La, Salvington, *tel.* (090671) 3823
Winslea Holiday Apartments, *tel.* (0903) 39795
Garages: Caffyns, Broadwater Rd, *tel.* (0903) 31111
Dagenham Motors, Mulberry La, Goring, *tel.* (0903) 504321
H G Steele & Son, Broadwater Trad Est, *tel.* (0903) 37527
West Sussex Motors, Palatine Rd, Goring-by-Sea, *tel.* (0903) 44972

Directory

ACTIVITIES AND SPORTS

ANGLING

Fishing opportunities in the region covered by this guide are particularly good, and the variety of its waters is more than adequate to satisfy the needs of specialists and all-round anglers alike.

Four major rivers – the Arun, Adur, Ouse and Cuckmere – are fed by an extensive pattern of tributaries ranging from small brooks to the more substantial Rother and Dudwell. The entire network offers excellent coarse fishing in attractive countryside, and esturial fishing may be enjoyed where the main rivers meet the sea. Some stretches are free public water, and some can be fished by day tickets – usually available from local tackle shops or angling societies.

None can be fished without a Southern Water Authority rod licence, which is obtainable from their Fisheries Office, *tel.* (0273) 596766. Full information regarding angling in the area is also available from that source, and most of the local tackle shops will advise on venues. Estuary fishing – yielding mullet and flatfish – is often subject to ticket purchase from the Harbour Master, or a similar authority. Again, the tackle and bait dealers will advise.

Still-water anglers are amply catered for by a good selection of lake fisheries, and game fishermen can choose from venues including reservoirs at Ardingly and Arlington.

Beach fishing is plentiful, there is also pier fishing at the resorts, and skippers offering deep-sea trips for parties are based at all the marinas. Those at Littlehampton and Brighton are particularly noted.

BOATING

Brighton boasts the largest marina in Europe. Undergoing major redevelopment at the time of publishing, it will also incorporate a health and sports centre, with a water theme park. Smaller marinas are at Newhaven, Shoreham Harbour and on the River Arun at Littlehampton and Ford.

There are also boat moorings in Littlehampton Harbour, where recreational craft mix with working vessels. Public launching facilities are at Littlehampton, Fishermans Hard and near Swan Bridge, in Pulborough.

At both Houghton and Arundel small boats are available for hire. For the less adventurous, a river cruiser operates during the summer months from Littlehampton to Arundel and Houghton Bridge.

The Southern Leisure Centre south of Chichester is based on a series of extensive water areas, offering water ski-ing and boating.

Brighton Marina
Tel. (0273) 693636
Littlehampton Marina
Tel. (0903) 713553
Newhaven Marina
Tel. (0273) 513881
Sealink (Dieppe Ferries)
Tel. (0273) 512266
Surrey Boat Yard
Tel. (0273) 461491

GOLF

Attractive and exacting courses can be found in surroundings varying from gentle rurality to exposed coastal dunes and windswept downland slopes. Many local clubs welcome visitors, but it is wise to check by 'phone before turning up. Details of most are listed in the *AA Guide to Golf Courses.*

RACING AND POLO

For the race goer there are three courses which offer top quality sport. On the flat, Goodwood is most famous for its meeting at the beginning of August, but there are a further 10 days racing there between May and October.

Fontwell Park is a most attractive jumping course with some 17 days of National Hunt fixtures between August and May each year. Brighton Racecourse, just outside the town, offers 17 days flat racing between April and October.

Polo is synonymous with Cowdray Park, and Prince Charles can often be seen playing his favourite sport on that ground.

Brighton Racecourse Race Hill
Tel. (0273) 603580
Cowdray Park Polo Club
Tel. (073081) 3257/2423
Fontwell Park Racecourse
Tel. (024368) 3335
Goodwood Racecourse Ltd
Tel. (0243) 774838

WALKING

Sussex, which has some of the best walking country in England, is known in particular for the South Downs Way long-distance footpath and bridleway from Old Winchester Hill in Hampshire to Eastbourne in East Sussex. The whole of the Way can be walked in four days, but a week or 10 days is a better proposition for most (see page 16). West Sussex County Council organises an eight-day walk of the South Downs Way every June, when over 200 people participate.

The County Council, with the support of parish councils and amenity groups, organises an annual guided walks programme entitled *Exploring West Sussex.* There are approximately 150 walks arranged each year between May and September, and each one is led by a voluntary guide who is well acquainted with the area.

Exploring the Sussex Downs is a leaflet of guided walks for all the family, produced jointly by East and West Sussex County Councils. Most of the walks take place at evenings and weekends and offer people who are not necessarily regular hikers the opportunity to take an enjoyable walk in the countryside.

The Downs Link bridges the gap between the North Downs Way at St Martha's Hill – near Guildford, in Surrey – and the South Downs Way, near Steyning in West Sussex. For the most part it follows the track of a disused railway line.

On a smaller scale is the Worth Way, a six-mile path following an old railway line from Three Bridges to East Grinstead. Copies of the leaflets mentioned and details of the South Downs Way can be obtained from the County Secretary, County Hall, Chichester. *Tel.* (0243) 777999.

CRAFTS

Coastal East and West Sussex in particular offer the type of environment in which craft enterprises thrive – and so do many of the picturesque villages inland.

Alfriston
JCJ Pottery, Drusillas. Throwing, turning and decorating of a wide range of stoneware, porcelain and house-name plates. By appointment all year. *Tel.* (0323) 870234

Arundel
Arundel Dial Service, 38 Maltravers Street. Restoration of damaged painted clock dials; also, resilvering of brass dials. By appointment all year. *Tel.* (0903) 882574
Country Crafts, The Street. Here visitors can watch furniture being made. Open all year, Monday to Saturday. *Tel.* (0243) 551387
Jacques Ruijterman, Castle Mews, Tarrant Street. Glass engraving by stipple, flexible drive and sand-blast.

By appointment all year (except Wednesdays). *Tel.* (0903) 883597

Bosham
Bosham Walk, Bosham Lane. Jewellery making, needlework, spinning, weaving, clock restoration and glass engraving. Open all year. *Tel.* (0243) 572475

Brighton
Beach Ceramics, Kings Road. Ceramics and raku work. By appointment all year. *Tel.* (0273) 725013
Brighton Open Studios, Edward Street. Screen-printing, photographic and autographic work. By appointment all year.
Dorothy Ablett (Crafts), Saltdean. Spinning, teasing, carding and weaving of wall-hangings, scarves, cushions, bedspreads and table-mats is demonstrated. By appointment all year. *Tel.* (0273) 32530
North Star Studios Ltd, Ditchling Road. Production of artist's prints, silk screens, etchings, lithographs and photographs. By appointment all year. *Tel.* (0273) 601041

Burgess Hill
Jack Trowbridge (Crafts), 75 Royal George Road. The making of silver jewellery, lettering in stone and ecclesiastical work demonstrated. By appointment all year.
Tel. (04446) 2208
Sheila Southwell Handpainted Porcelain, Garden Studio, 7 West Street. China and porcelain decorated by hand and kiln-fired. Restoration work also undertaken. By appointment all year.
Tel. (04446) 44307

Chichester
Donnington Pottery, Blacksmiths Cottage, Selsey Road. Throwing, packing, firing, glazing and decorating of stoneware pottery.

Eastbourne
Beckhurst Glass, The Pier. Here the complete process of making glass models on teak bases can be watched. Open all year.
Tel. (0323) 870023
Isobel Kennett Crafts, Rise Park Gardens. Pillow-lace crochet, broomstick, tatting, hairpin and Teneriffe lace work demonstrated. By appointment all year (excluding June and August).
Tel. (0323) 764717

Hailsham
Wartling Pottery. Throwing, turning and glazing of domestic stoneware pottery and lamp bases. Open all year. *Tel.* (0323) 833145

Hassocks
Recollect Studio, The Old School, London Road, Sayers Common. Porcelain dolls and dolls' house miniatures made. *Tel.* (0273) 681862

Haywards Heath
The Blacksmiths Shop, Horsted Keynes. Construction and forging of

ornamental ironwork and general smithing. Open all year.
Tel. (0342) 810292

Heathfield
Audrey Jarett Crafts, Dallington. Hessian sculptures and traditional dolls made. By appointment all year. *Tel.* (042482) 233

Henfield
Harwoods Farm, West End Lane. Specialist turning of salad bowls and platters in all English hardwoods. By appointment all year.
Tel. (0273) 492820

Herstmonceux
Sussex Windsors, Windmill Hill. Windsor chairs and tables in English hardwoods made. By appointment all year. *Tel.* (0323) 832388
The Truggery, Coopers Croft. Clearing, shaving-up, steaming and nailing of traditional Sussex trug baskets, made from chestnut and willow. Open all year.
Tel. (0323) 832314

Lewes
Mary Potter Studio, Laughton. Batik pictures, screen-printed scarves and cards made. By appointment all year. *Tel.* (082584) 438
The Old Needlemakers, West Street. Embroidery, quilting, spinning and weaving, picture framing and textile painting. Open all year.

Lower Dicker
Peartree Pottery, Lower Hackhurst Farm. Handthrown domestic stoneware pottery, some glazing and decorating work. Open all year.

Pevensey
Glynleigh Studio, Westham. Restoration of antiques and modern work in copper, brass and bronze. By appointment all year.
Tel. (0323) 763456

INFORMATION CENTRES

Full tourist information is available from the centres detailed in the following list. See also the *Directory* entry *Useful Addresses*.

Arundel
61 High Street. *Tel.* (0903) 882268
Bognor Regis
Belmont Street. *Tel.* (0243) 823140

Brighton
Marlborough House, 54 Old Steine. *Tel.* (0273) 23755/27560 (Seafront, Kings Road. *Tel.* (0273) 23755)
Chichester
St Peters Market, West Street. *Tel.* (0243) 775888
Eastbourne
3, Cornfield Terrace. *Tel.* (0323) 27474/21333 *Ext* 1184/1187. (Terminus Road Precinct. [0323] 21333 *Ext* 1184/1187. Seafront [0323] 647724)
Hailsham
Hailsham Library, Western Road. *Tel.* (0323) 840604
Hove
Town Hall, Norton Road. *Tel.* (0273) 775400
Lewes
32 High Street. *Tel.* (0273) 471600
Littlehampton
Windmill Theatre, Coastguards Road. *Tel.* (0903) 713480
Seaford
Station Approach. *Tel.* (0323) 897426
Shoreham-by-Sea
86 High Street. *Tel.* (07917) 2086
Worthing
Town Hall, Chapel Road. *Tel.* (0903) 210022/39999 *Ext* 132/3

PLACES TO VISIT

This section is a condensed, easy-reference guide to major attractions listed under place-name headings in the main gazetteer. Included are houses and castles, parks and gardens, museums and art galleries – and various outdoor attractions. It is wise to 'phone before visiting, to check that conditions of entry have not changed.

HOUSES AND CASTLES

Alfriston Clergy House (NT). Adjoining St Andrew's Church on the Tye, this 14th-century thatched and timber-framed house was built for a group of parish priests in the time of Chaucer. It was the first building acquired by the National Trust. Open Good Friday to end of October.
Tel. (0323) 870001

Alfriston Clergy House, built of oak framing filled with wattle and daub

Arundel Castle.
Ancestral home of the Dukes of Norfolk for over 700 years. Much was rebuilt at the end of the 19th century, but the 11th-century keep and ancient barbican tower remain. Contains furniture, paintings and armour. Open afternoons Monday to Friday and every Sunday, April to October. *Tel.* (0903) 882173

Bateman's (NT) *(1m SW of Burwash)*.
Former home of Rudyard Kipling, this lovely 17th-century house has attractive gardens and a working water-mill. Open April to October, Saturday to Wednesday.
Tel. (0435) 882302

Danny *Hurstpierpoint*.
Dignified Elizabethan brick mansion of 1595, enlarged and restored in 1728. Acquired by the Mutual Households Association in 1956, it still retains paintings and furniture on loan from the Campion family and provides 26 private apartments. Open to the public Wednesdays and Thursdays May to September.
Tel. (0273) 833000

Firle Place *Firle*.
Home of the Gage family for over 500 years. Contains a notable collection of Old Masters, porcelain and furniture. Open June to September Sunday, Wednesday and Thursday. Also bank holidays.
Tel. (079159) 335

Glynde Place *Glynde*.
Elizabethan manor house with mid 18th-century alterations. Open June to September, Wednesday and Thursday afternoons.
Tel. (079159) 248

Goodwood House *near Chichester*.
Imposing seat of the Dukes of Richmond since 1697 and frequently visited by Royalty for Goodwood Races. Contains a famous collection of works of art. Open Easter Sunday and Monday, Sundays and Mondays May to September. Also Tuesdays, Wednesdays and Thursdays in August. Closed event days.
Tel. (0243) 774107

Lancing College.
Famous school founded by Nathaniel Woodard in 1848. Stands conspicuously on a ridge of the Downs overlooking the River Adur. The majestic chapel has only just been completed. The school buildings siding two quadrangles are a notable example of Gothic Revival style. *Tel.* (0273) 452213

Michelham Priory *Upper Dicker, Hailsham (off A22 and A27)*.
Founded in 1229 for Augustinian Canons. Situated in six acres of gardens surrounded by a large moat and approached through an imposing 14th-century gatehouse. In 1587 the Pelham family converted the refectory and added a Tudor wing to the house. Also physic garden, working water-mill and Tudor barn. Open daily March to October. *Tel.* (0323) 844224

Newtimber Place *Hassocks*.
A 17th-century moated house at the foot of the South Downs, with Etruscan style wall paintings in the hall, and gardens with a Georgian dovecote. Open Thursdays May to August. *Tel.* (0273) 833104

Parham House *near Pulborough*.
Beautiful Elizabethan family home with fine gardens standing in a deer park. The house contains a fine collection of paintings, furniture, carpets and rare needlework. Open Easter to October Wednesday, Thursday, Saturday, Sunday and bank holiday afternoons.
Tel. (090 66) 2021

Petworth House (NT).
Magnificent 17th-century home of the Wyndham family. The pictures, including important works by Van Dyck and Turner (a frequent visitor), comprise one of the finest private collections to be seen in England. Grinling Gibbons carvings, sculpture gallery and 13th-century chapel. Open April to end of October, daily Mondays to Fridays. *Tel.* (0798) 42207

Preston Manor *Preston Road, Brighton*.
Edwardian house with walled garden featuring a pets' cemetery. Open daily except Monday, but open bank holiday Mondays. *Tel.* (0273) 603005 *Ext 59*

Priest House *West Hoathly*.
This fine example of a typical 15th-century timber-framed house serves as a focal point for the attractive Wealden village. The museum it houses aims to give an impression of village life during the 18th to 19th centuries. Open April to October, Tuesday to Sunday and bank holiday Mondays.
Tel. (0342) 810479

St Mary's *Bramber*.
Regarded as the best example in Sussex of a late 15th-century timber-framed house. Ten rooms on view, including one with rare Elizabethan painted panelling. Collection of handicrafts and exhibition of antiques. Open April to October. *Tel.* (0903) 816205

St Mary's Hospital *Chichester*.
One of the most interesting of many ancient buildings in Chichester. Late 13th century, these almshouses are still used for their original purpose. May be visited daily, except Sundays and Mondays, October to March. *Tel.* (0243) 783377

Stansted Park *Rowlands Castle*.
Family seat of the Earl and Countess of Bessborough, set in parkland. Inside can be seen the blue Drawing Room, the Dining Room, the classically elegant Hall and the restored old kitchen. John Keats wrote some of his finest verse in the chapel. Open May to September. *Tel.* (070 541) 2265

Uppark (NT) *South Harting*.
This splendid late 17th-century house stands high on the Downs and remains essentially unchanged since Sir Matthew Featherstonhaugh furnished it in 1750. Fine furniture and plasterwork. Grand Tour pictures, Queen Anne dolls' house. Open April to end September, Wednesday, Thursday, Sunday and bank holiday Mondays.
Tel. (073 085) 317

Wilmington Priory *near Polegate*.
Priory remains and 18th-century farmhouse with a museum specialising in old agricultural equipment. Open March to October daily except Tuesday. *Tel.* (0323) 870537

MUSEUMS AND ART GALLERIES

Amberley Chalk Pits Museum *(off the B2139 between Storrington and the A29)*.
Working open-air museum, where the industrial history of south-east England is being studied and preserved, based on lime-burning kilns situated in a large chalk quarry. Other industries are being brought on to the site. Open Wednesday to Sunday from late March to late October.
Tel. (079 881) 370

Arundel Museum and Heritage Centre.
Numerous models and exhibits dealing with the archaeological, agricultural, architectural, industrial and cultural development of the town and its environment. Open Tuesday to Saturday, Easter to October. *Tel.* (0903) 882268
Toy and Military Museum.
A collection of toys including dolls, lead and tin toys, dolls'-house furniture and rocking horses, from the 18th century to the present. Open most days, Easter to October, daily in July and August.
Tel. (0903) 883101/882908

Bramber *House of Pipes*.
The world's only 'smokiana' exhibition, with 25,000 items from 150 countries covering 1,500 years. Wheelchairs welcome. Open all year except Christmas Day.
Tel. (0903) 812122

Brighton
Booth Museum of Natural History.
British birds mounted in natural settings. Open daily except Thursday. *Tel.* (0273) 552586
Museum and Art Gallery.
Displays of Art Nouveau and Art Deco furniture. Fashion Gallery, Sussex archaeology, pottery and

porcelain. *Tel.* (0273) 31004
Royal Pavilion.
George IV's unique seaside palace.
Much of the original furniture has
been returned on loan from HM
The Queen. Open daily.
Tel. (0273) 603005

Chichester District Museum.
Housed in a converted 18th-century
corn store, its collections illustrate
the history of the city and district
from the Stone Age to the present
day. Temporary exhibitions held
regularly. Open Tuesday to Saturday
all year. *Tel.* (0243) 784683
Guildhall Museum, Priory Park.
Formerly the choir of the
Franciscan church, later used as a
Guildhall. Displays archaeological
discoveries from Chichester and
district, including particularly fine
Roman exhibits. Open Tuesday to
Saturday, June to September.
Tel. (0243) 784683
Mechanical Music and Doll Collection.
Barrel organs, musical boxes,
polyphons, and dance and fair
organs fully restored and working.
Also, Victorian dolls, magic lantern,
veteran cycles, motor cycles and
natural-history exhibits. Open daily,
Easter to September. Saturdays and
Sundays, October to Easter.
Tel. (0243) 785421
Pallant House Gallery.
The recently-restored Gallery was
built in 1713 by Henry 'Lisbon'
Peckham, and now houses the
Hussey collection of paintings,
drawings and sculpture ranging
from Durer to Henry Moore.
Period rooms. Exhibitions. Open
Tuesday to Saturday all the year.
Tel. (0243) 774557

Eastbourne *Coastal Defence Museum.*
Martello Tower with displays of
19th-century defence methods and
equipment. Open Easter to October.
Tel. (0323) 33952
Redoubt Fortress.
Home of the Sussex Combined
Services Museum and the
Regimental Museum of the Royal
Sussex Regiment. Also an aquarium.
Open Easter to November daily.
Tel. (0323) 33952
*Towner Art Gallery and Local History
Museum.*
Georgian manor house with
displays of Eastbourne's history and
British works of art. Open all year;
closed Mondays in winter.
Tel. (0323) 21635/25112

Horsham Museum, *Causeway
House.*
Varied collection includes toys,
folklife, costumes, local bygones and
aspects of town life. Open Tuesday
to Saturday all year.
Tel. (0403) 54959

Hove *British Engineerium
(off the A27).*
Hundreds of model and full-size
engines brought to life. In steam
every Sunday and on Public
Holidays. Open daily.
Tel. (0273) 559583

Lancing, *College Museum (off the
A27).*
This is a typical small college
collection with three main
categories: local finds; items
illustrative of the college's history;
and objects from many periods and
places given by old boys and friends
of the school. Open daily during
term time only.
Tel. (0273) 452213

Lewes *Anne of Cleves' House.*
Attractive rambling building
containing domestic bygones,
Sussex ironwork and a history
gallery. Open mid February to mid
November, also Sunday afternoon
April to October. *Tel.* (0273)
474610
Castle and Barbican House Museum.
Norman castle and fascinating
museum of exhibits from the Sussex
Archaeological Society's collection.
Open daily April to October.
Tel. (0273) 474379

Littlehampton Museum *12a River
Road.*
Nautical and maritime exhibits
illustrating the story of the port and
boat-building industry. Collection of
maps of harbour. Open Tuesday to
Saturday, summer; Thursday to
Saturday, winter. *Tel.* (0903)
715149

Rottingdean *Grange Museum and
Art Gallery.*
Includes Kipling exhibits and part of
the National Toy Museum.
Frequent temporary exhibitions.
Open daily except Wednesday and
Sunday. *Tel.* (0273) 31004

Royal Greenwich Observatory
*Herstmonceux Castle (10m N of
Eastbourne, between A27 and A271).*
Displays about astronomy and the
wonders of the universe, from
Halley's Comet to black holes.
Telescopes, video theatre and
souvenir shop. All set in 300 acres
of gardens and grounds with picnic
spots, nature trail and tea shop.
Herstmonceux Castle houses small
historical exhibition, and parts are
open on selected weekends. Open
Good Friday to end September.
Tel. (0323) 833171

Shoreham-by-Sea *Marlipins
Museum.*
This is one of the oldest secular
buildings in Sussex, with a
distinctive chequered front of flint
and stone. It contains an interesting
collection of local relics, geological
items, paintings, ship models,
photographs and maps relating to
the port of Shoreham and the
maritime history of the area.
Open end of April to September.
Tel. (07917) 62994

**Tangmere Military Aviation
Museum.**
A display of models, maps,
photographs, uniforms, documents
and aircraft relics which give the
history of this famous RAF Station

and the Battle of Britain. There is
also a restored Hawker Hunter jet
fighter. Open every day, March to
October. *Tel.* (0243) 775223

**Worthing Museum and Art
Gallery.**
The archaeology, geology and
history of the locality are illustrated
here, and there is a large collection
of costumes. Important Anglo-
Saxon items from Highdown.
Frequent temporary exhibitions in
Art Gallery. Also, English pottery,
porcelain and glass. Open daily
except Sundays.
Tel. (0903) 39999

OUTDOOR ATTRACTIONS

Arundel Wildfowl Trust.
Some 55 acres between the River
Arun and Swanbourne Lake.
Landscaped pens, lakes and
paddocks contain ducks, geese and
swans from all over the world, as
well as wild birds attracted to the
refuge. Hides. Open every day
except Christmas Day.
Tel. (0903) 883355

**Bentley Wildfowl Reserve and
Motor Museum** *Halland.*
Around 1,000 birds in 100-acre
countryside setting. Motor Museum
houses vintage, Edwardian and
veteran vehicles. Bentley House has
antique furniture and paintings of
wildfowl. Also formal gardens.
Open March to September.
Weekends in winter except January.
Tel. (082 584) 573

Bignor Roman Villa.
Celebrated Roman site with some
of the finest mosaic pavements in
the country. Museum with models,
pictures and objects found on the
site. Open March to October.
Closed Mondays except August and
Bank Holidays. *Tel.* (079 87) 259

Bluebell Railway, The.
(Sheffield Park & Horsted Keynes).
Bluebell Railway operates vintage
steam trains between Sheffield Park
and Horsted Keynes. Collection of
historic locomotives and museum to
view. Trains run on Sunday in
January, February and December
(and Boxing Day). Special events
held annually. Saturday and Sunday
in March, April and November.
Wednesday, Saturday and Sunday
in May and October. Daily June to
September inclusive bank holidays
and Easter week.
Tel. (082 572) 2370

Butterfly Centre,
Royal Parade, Eastbourne.
Beautifully landscaped gardens full
of exotic plants, shrubs and trees.
There are butterflies, on the paths,
flowers, bushes and trees. Open
from Palm Sunday to the end of
October. *Tel.* (0323) 645522

Drusillas Zoo Park *near Alfriston.*
Good small zoo with rare breeds,

adventure playground, butterfly house, crafts and a bakery. Open daily all year, except Christmas. *Tel.* (0323) 870234

Fishbourne Roman Palace *near Chichester.*
Discovered in 1960 and since excavated in great detail. This is probably the most famous and extensive Roman site on view in Britain. Mosaic floors and foundations of one wing have been covered for preservation. Open all year. *Tel.* (0243) 785859

Kingley Vale National Nature Reserve *near West Stoke.*
Much of the reserve is open to the public, and can be explored by several rights of way. Permits are required for some areas. Applications for permits should be made to South East Regional Office, NCC, Zealds, Church Street, Wye, Ashford, Kent, TN25 5BW.

Living World Museum
Seven Sisters Country Park, Exceat.
Living displays from countryside and seashore, with a choice according to season from exotic silkmoths, tropical butterfles, hairy tarantulas, an observation bee-hive, marine and freshwater aquaria. Open daily March to November. *Tel.* (0323) 870100

Shipley Windmill *(between Horsham and Storrington).*
Working smock-mill, built in 1879 and restored in 1957 in memory of Hilaire Belloc, the writer who owned it. *Tel.* (040 387) 310

Spring Hill Wildfowl
Cranes, flamingoes, rheas, white peacocks, pheasants, geese and ducks. One of the finest collections in the country. Open daily. *Tel.* (034 282) 2783

Weald and Downland Open Air Museum *Singleton.*
On a 40-acre site on the West Dean Estate north of Chichester. Ancient buildings threatened with destruction have been moved and re-erected. Picnic site and beautiful setting. Open April to October daily. November to March, Sundays and Wednesdays. *Tel.* (024 363) 348

Woods Mill *Henfield.*
Headquarters of the Sussex Trust for Nature Conservation. Education Centre, field museum, lecture rooms, nature trail and 15-acre nature reserve. Open April to September Tuesdays, Wednesdays, Thursdays and Saturdays. *Tel.* (0273) 492630

PARKS AND GARDENS

A feature about gardens in the South Downs region begins on page 27. Some are open only on a few select days when their owners judge that the garden will be at its peak.

For up-to-date information on opening dates and times of gardens, reference should be made to the current edition of *Gardens of England & Wales Open to the Public* – available from The National Gardens Scheme, 57 Lower Belgrave Street, London SW1W 0LR (or booksellers). Fuller information on National Trust properties (NT) is given in the annual *National Trust Handbook* – free to members of the Trust or available for purchase from booksellers or The National Trust, 36 Queen Anne's Gate, London SW1H 9AS.

Borde Hill Garden *(1½m N of Haywards Heath on Balcombe Road).*
Large garden, rare trees and shrubs, view, woodland walk. Open March to October, Tuesday, Wednesday, Thursday, Saturday, Sunday and all bank holidays. *Tel.* (0444) 450326

Buchan Country Park *(off the A264 Crawley to Horsham road).*
About 160 acres of woodlands and glades with two ponds for fishing. Day tickets available. Information centre open at weekends.

Denmans Garden *Fontwell.*
Original 3½-acre garden developed over the last 30 years. Planned with an emphasis on shape, colour and texture. Conservatories, water garden, country shop and plant centre. Open April to November, Wednesday, Sunday and bank holidays. *Tel.* (024 368) 2808

Highdown *(N off A259 between Worthing and Littlehampton).*
Laid out in a chalk pit with lovely views from Highdown Hill. Open all year Monday to Friday also weekends and bank holidays April to September. *Tel.* (0903) 501054

Hollygate Cactus Nursery *Ashington.*
Unique collection of over 20,000 plants, many rare specimens from the more arid areas of the world. Attractively landscaped garden and glasshouses. Open every day except Christmas. *Tel.* (0903) 892930

Leonardslee *(4½m SE of Horsham on A281).*
Extensive spring flowering shrubs, rhododendrons, azaleas, set by several lakes, valley filled with camellia. Open every day, April to June and every weekend in summer. *Tel.* (040 376) 212

Nymans Gardens *Handcross (4½m S of Crawley on B2114).*
Walled garden, shrubs, herbaceous borders, sunk garden set in 30 acres. Open April to October daily except Mondays and Fridays. Also open bank holidays.

Parham Gardens *near Pulborough (A283 W of Storrington).*
Walled garden and pleasure ground. Open Easter to October, Wednesday, Thursday, Saturday,

Sunday and bank holidays. *Tel.* (090 66) 2021

Sheffield Park Garden (NT)
(5m E of Haywards Heath off A275).
Magnificent 150-acre gardens with lake. Open April to November daily except Monday, but open bank holidays. *Tel.* (0825) 790655

Tilgate Park *Crawley.*
A 400-acre park owned by Horsham District Council, with many rare trees. The Nature Centre

Flowering cacti can be seen all year at Hollygate Nursery, Ashington

has many rare breeds of domestic animals and is open every day of the year (except Christmas day, Boxing day and New Year's day). There are three fishing lakes in the park as well as an 18-hole golf course. The park is open from dawn to dusk daily. *Tel.* (0293) 21168

Wakehurst Place (NT) *(1m NW of Ardingly on B2028).*
Important collection of exotic trees, shrubs, picturesque watercourse including several lakes and ponds in over 100 acres, leased to the Royal Botanic Gardens at Kew. Formal gardens and island beds are arranged round the part Elizabethan House. Open daily all year, except Christmas and New Year's Day. *Tel.* (0444) 892701

West Dean Gardens *(on A286, 6m N of Chichester).*
Some 35 acres of trees and shrubs, with garden history exhibition, picnic and play area. Open April to September. Applehouse Nursery, sells shrubs and plants, open all year. *Tel.* (024 363) 301

CALENDAR OF EVENTS

January
Holiday on Ice, Brighton
Exhibition: Lifestyle, Eastbourne

February
South East Counties Antiques
 Dealers' Fair, Goodwood House

March
Exhibition: Modelworld, Brighton
 Centre

April
International Clown Convention,
 Bognor Regis
Southern Garden Show, Brighton
 Centre
Brighton Marina 10k International
 Road Race
Ardingly Antiques and Collectors
 Fair (spring)
British Coach Rally, Brighton
Cowdray Park Polo Club Season

May
Chichester Festival Theatre Season
 (May to September)
Eastbourne International Folk
 Festival
Brighton Festival
Festival of Family Fun, Brighton
Historic Commercial Vehicle Run,
 Brighton
Gatwick South of England Horse
 Trials, Ardingly
MG Regency Run, Brighton
Royal Escape Yacht Race, Brighton
Glyndebourne Festival Opera
 Season (May to August)
Showjumping: The Everest Double
 Glazing Nations Cup, Hickstead
Bowling: EBA Gateway Masters
 Tournament

June
Brighton Motor and Leisure Show
South of England Show, Ardingly
Tennis: Pilkington Glass Ladies
 International Championships
Heavy Horse Demonstration,
 Singleton
London to Brighton Bike Ride

July
Chichester Festivities
European Dressage Championships,
 Goodwood House
Showjumping: The Dubar Cup,
 Hickstead
Tennis: The Prudential County

Cup International Tournament,
 Eastbourne
Festival of Pub Games and Real
 Ale, Midhurst
Showjumping: The Silk Cup
 Derby, Hickstead

August
Cricket Week, Eastbourne
Brighton Carnival Week
CAMRA Great British Beer Festival,
 Brighton
Grand Arun Charity Bath Tub Race
EBA Gateway National Bowling
 Championships, Worthing
British Craft and Hobby Fair,
 Brighton Centre
Hove Festival Cricket Week
International Birdman Rally,
 Bognor Regis Pier
Eastbourne Show

*Final stages of the RAC London to
Brighton Veteran Car Run*

All Star Country Music Festival,
 Worthing
Arundel Festival

September
English Vineyard Wine Festival,
 Alfriston
Ardingly Antiques and Collector's
 Fair (autumn)

October
Tennis: Pretty Polly Classic
 Tournament, Brighton Centre
Steam Threshing and Autumn
 Ploughing with Horses and
 Vintage Tractors, Singleton
Chiddingly Festival

November
RAC London to Brighton Veteran
 Car Run
Bonfire Celebrations, Lewes
British Craft and Gift Fair, Brighton
 Centre

USEFUL ADDRESSES

Details of Information Centres in
the region are contained in a
separate section within this
Directory. Additional information
for visitors can be obtained from
local tourist board offices and
local authorities.

**Camping and Caravan Club of
Great Britain,**
11 Grosvenor Place, London
SW1W 0EY.
Tel. (01 828) 1012/7

Countryside Commission,
South East Regional Office,
30/32 Southampton Street,
London WC2E 7RA.
Tel. (01 240) 2771
National Trust,
Southern Recreational Office,
Polesden Lacey,
Dorking, Surrey.
Tel. (0372) 53401
Nature Conservancy Council,
The Old Candlemakers,
West Street,
Lewes BN7 2NZ.
Tel. (0273) 476595

South East England Tourist Board,
1 Warwick Park,
Tunbridge Wells,
Kent TN2 5TA.
Tel. (0892) 40766
Southern Water Authority,
Guilbourne House,
Chatsworth Road,
Worthing.
Tel. (0903) 205252
Youth Hostels Association,
St Stephen's Hill,
St Albans
A11 2DY.
Tel. (0727) 55215

SOUTH DOWNS

Atlas

The following pages contain a legend, key map and
the South Downs atlas, three motor tours
and sixteen coast and downland walks.

Above: Birling Gap

South Downs Legend

TOURIST INFORMATION

⚊	Camp Site	🐑	Nature reserve
🚐	Caravan Site	☆	Other tourist feature
ℹ	Information Centre	🚂	Preserved railway
P	Parking Facilities	🐎	Racecourse
☀	Viewpoint	♈	Wildlife park
✕	Picnic site	🏛	Museum
⚑	Golf course or links	🐾	Nature or forest trail
🏰	Castle	ᛗ	Ancient monument
🏚	Cave	℮ ℮	Telephones : public or motoring organisations
🏛	Country park	PC	Public Convenience
✿	Garden	▲	Youth Hostel
🏠	Historic house		

▬ ▬   ▪ ▪ ▪ ▪   Waymarked Path / Long Distance Path / Recreational Path

ORIENTATION

True North
At the centre of the area is 1°14'W of Grid North

Magnetic North
At the centre of the area is about 6° W of Grid North in 1988 decreasing by about ½° in three years

Diagrammatic Only

GRID REFERENCE SYSTEM

The map references used in this book are based on the Ordnance Survey National Grid, correct to within 1000 Metres They comprise two letters and four figures, and are preceded by the atlas page number.

Thus the reference for Brighton appears 86 TQ 3105

86 is the atlas page number

TQ identifies the major (100km) grid square concerned (see diag)

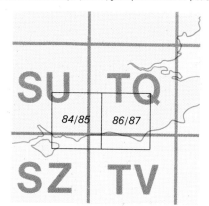

3105 locates the lower left-hand corner of the kilometre grid square in which Brighton appears

Take the first figure of the reference 3, this refers to the numbered grid running along the bottom of the page. Having found this line, the second figure 1, tells you the distance to move in tenths to the right of this line. A vertical line through this point is the first half of the reference.

The third figure 0, refers to the numbered grid lines on the right hand side of the page, finally the fourth figure 5, indicates the distance to move in tenths above this line. A horizontal line drawn through this point to intersect with the first line gives the precise location of the places in question.

KEY-MAP 1:500,000 or 8 MILES to 1"

ROAD INFORMATION

Motorway with service area, service area (limited access) and junction with junction number

Motorway junction with limited interchange

Motorway, service area and junction under construction with proposed opening date *Mid 1988*

Primary routes } Single and dual carriageway with service area
Main Road

Main Road under construction

Narrow Road with passing places

Other roads { B roads (majority numbered) / Unclassified (selected) }   *B 2116*

Gradient (1 in 7 and steeper) and toll   *TOLL*

Primary routes and main roads } Mileages are shown on the map between large markers and between small markers in large and small type

Motorways } 1 mile = 1·61 kilometres

Primary Routes
These form a national network of recommended through routes which complement the motorway system. Selected places of major traffic importance are known as Primary Route Destinations and are shown on these maps thus CRAWLEY. This relates to the directions on road signs which on Primary Routes have a green background. To travel on a Primary Route, follow the direction to the next Primary Destination shown on the greenbacked road signs. On these maps Primary Route road numbers and mileages are shown in green

Motorways
A similar situation occurs with motorway routes where numbers and mileages, shown in blue on these maps correspond to the blue background of motorway road signs.

GENERAL FEATURES

Passenger railways (selected in conurbations)

AA..A RAC..R PO..T   Telephone call box

+·+·+·+·+·+·+·+·+·+·+   National Boundary

------------------   County or Region Boundary

✈   ○   Large Town Town / Village

⊕ ....   Airport

427.   Height (metres)

WATER FEATURES

By Sea { Internal ferry route / External ferry route }

Ferry.................   Short ferry routes for vehicles are annotated   Ferry

——————   Canal

Coastline, river and lake

ATLAS 1:200,000 or 3 MILES to 1"
TOURS 1:250,000 or 4 MILES to 1"

ROADS   Not necessarily rights of way

M 23	Motorway with service area and junction with junction number
A 27(T) Dual Carriageway	Trunk road
A 24 Dual Carriageway	Main road
A 24 Dual Carriageway	Roundabout or multiple level junction
B 2116 Dual Carriageway	Secondary road
	Other tarred road
	Other minor road
	Gradient 1 in 7 and steeper

RAILWAYS

	Road crossing under or over standard gauge track
	Level crossing
	Station
	Narrow gauge track

WATER FEATURES

Cliff, Slopes, Flat rock, Short ferry routes for vehicles, Transport for vehicles, Lake, Bridge, Ferry, Low water mark, Canal, Dunes, High water mark

ANTIQUITIES

	Native fortress
------	Roman road (course of)
Castle •	Other antiquities
CANOVIVM •	Roman antiquity

GENERAL FEATURES

	Buildings
	Wood
☎	Telephones : public or motoring organisations
⊕	Civil aerodrome (with custom facilities)
	Radio or TV mast
	Lighthouse

RELIEF

Feet	Metres	
		.274
		Heights in feet above mean sea level
3000	914	
2000	610	
1400	427	
		Contours at 200 ft intervals
1000	305	
600	183	
200	61	
		To convert feet to metres multiply by 0.3048
0	0	

WALKS 1:25,000 or 2½" to 1 MILE
ROADS AND PATHS   Not necessarily rights of way

M 23	Motorway
A 27(T)	Trunk road
A 24	Main road — Narrow roads with passing places are annotated
B 2224	Secondary road
A 24	Dual carriageway
	Road generally over 4m wide
	Road generally under 4m wide
	Other road, drive or track .... Path

RAILWAYS

	Multiple track		Level crossing
	Single track		Cutting
	Narrow Gauge		Embankment
	Road over & under		Tunnel
	Siding		

GENERAL FEATURES

♦	Church — with tower	Electricity transmission line
♦	or — with spire	pylon pole
+	Chapel — without tower or spire	
	Gravel pit	NT — National Trust always open
	Sand pit	NT — National Trust opening restricted
	Chalk pit, clay pit or quarry	FC — Forestry Commission pedestrians only (observe local signs)
	Refuse or slag heap	National Park

HEIGHTS AND ROCK FEATURES

Contours are at various metres vertical intervals

50 ·	Determined	ground survey
285 ·	by	air survey

*Surface heights are to the nearest metre / foot above mean sea level.
Heights shown close to a triangulation pillar refer to the station
height at ground level and not necessarily to the summit.*

Vertical Face

Loose rock   Boulders   Outcrop   Scree

75
60
50

PUBLIC RIGHTS OF WAY

*Public rights of way shown in this guide may not be evident
on the ground*

----------	Public Paths	Footpath
————		Bridleway
+++++	By-way open to all traffic	
-+-+-+-	Road used as a public path	

*Public rights of way indicated by these symbols have been derived from
Definitive Maps as amended by later enactments or instruments held by
Ordnance Survey between 1st August 1978 and 1st January 1985 and are
shown subject to the limitations imposed by the scale of mapping.*

Later information may be obtained from the appropriate County Council.

**The representation on this map of any other road, track or path
is no evidence of the existence of a right of way.**

WALKS AND TOURS (All Scales)

7 🥾	Start point of walk
→	Route of walk
	Line of walk
3 🚗	Start point of tour
→	Route of tour
	Featured tour

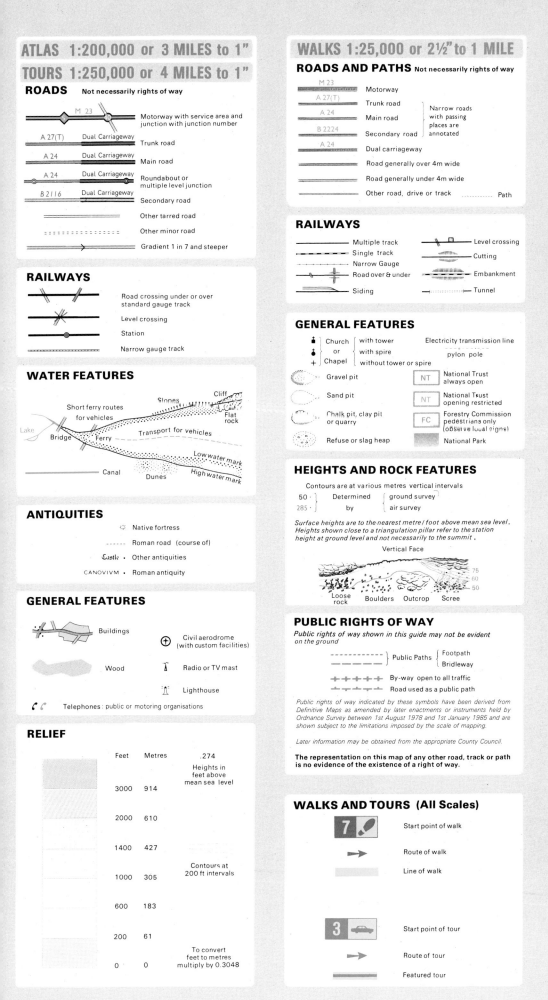

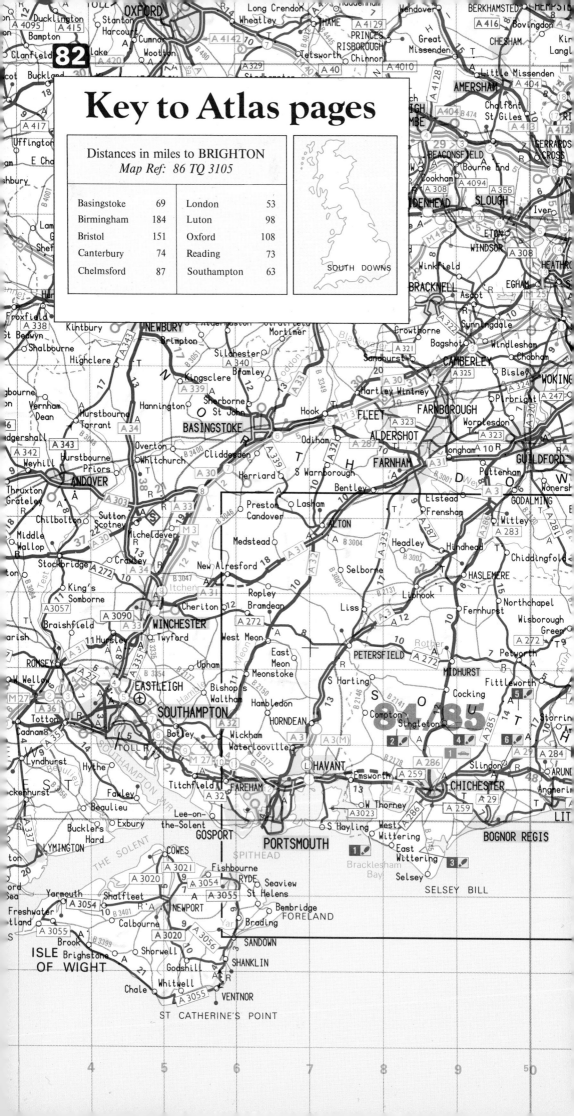

Key to Atlas pages

Distances in miles to BRIGHTON
Map Ref: 86 TQ 3105

Basingstoke	69	London	53
Birmingham	184	Luton	98
Bristol	151	Oxford	108
Canterbury	74	Reading	73
Chelmsford	87	Southampton	63

SOUTH DOWNS

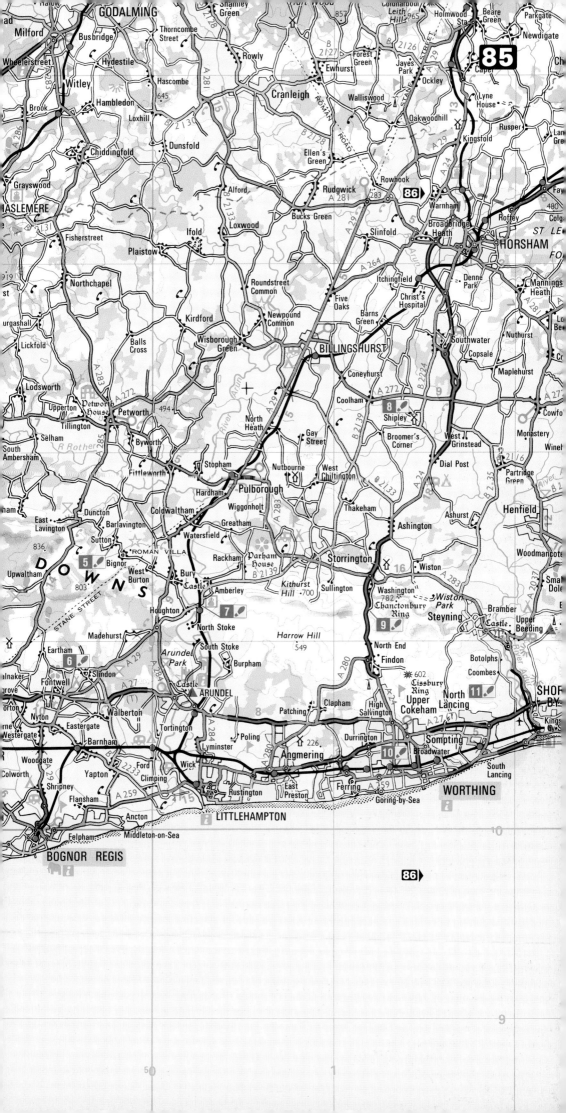

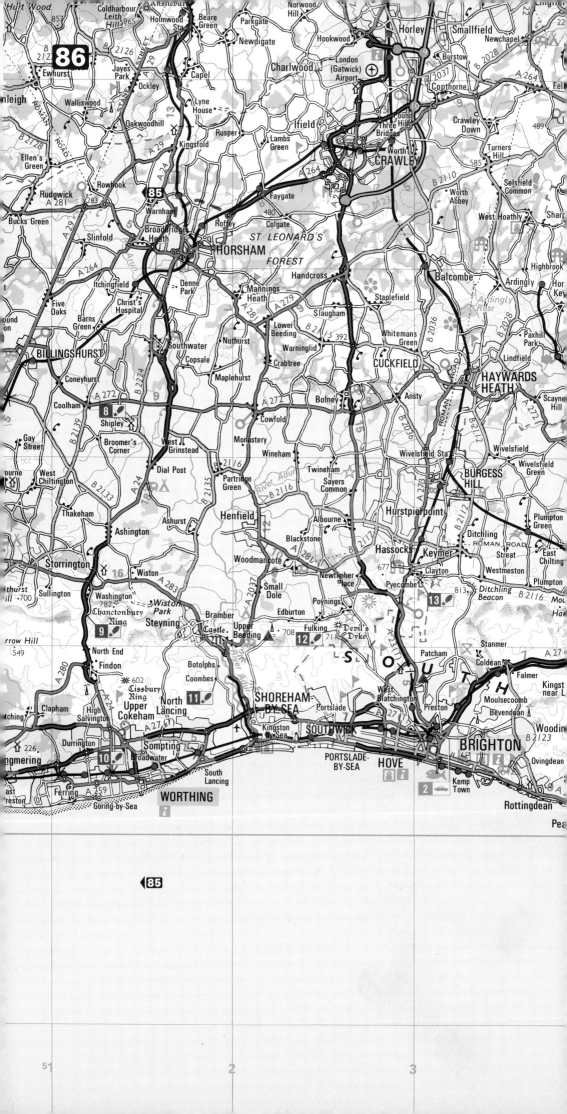

TOUR 1 53 MILES

A Sussex History Tour

There are many places of historical interest which may be visited during this drive – a Roman villa, a Norman castle, a medieval town, a stately home, an aviation museum and an open-air museum of traditional buildings from the area.

The drive starts from Chichester (see page 40), a beautiful city dating back to Roman times.

From the eastern side of the ring road follow signs for Bognor Regis A259, and at the Four Chestnuts public house keep forward (no sign) into Oving Road (the B2144). In ½ mile, at the traffic-lights, go forward across the Chichester bypass, signed Oving. In another ½ mile keep forward again, unclassified, signed Tangmere. Just over a mile farther bear left. Pass (right) the famous World War II fighter airfield of Tangmere. Now disused, it is the site of the Military Aviation Museum (see Chichester, page 40).

At the end of Tangmere village turn right on to the main A27 Worthing road. After a further 3 miles pass the edge of Fontwell – famous for its racecourse (diversion due to open in 1988) – and 4 miles farther at the roundabout take the second exit, unclassified, to enter the interesting town of Arundel (see page 34). The imposing, much-restored Norman castle is the ancestral home of the Dukes of Norfolk. Other notable buildings are the 19th-century Roman Catholic cathedral and 14th-century church of St Nicholas.

Return to the roundabout junction with the A27 to continue the main tour. Here take the exit signed London/Dorking to leave by the A284. Ascend through woodland (skirting the Arundel Castle estate on the right) and after 2½ miles at the roundabout take the third exit, B2139, signed Storrington (see page 66). There are pleasant views as the drive descends into the Arun Valley at Houghton. The river is crossed prior to Amberley Station, beyond which is the Amberley Chalkpits Museum (right). Shortly pass the turning to the attractive village of Amberley on the left (see page 32).

Continue along the foot of the Downs to reach Storrington. Here turn left on to the A283, signed Petworth and Pulborough. One mile farther pass the entrance to Parham House Gardens (see page 58). In another mile turn left on to an unclassified road, signed Greatham, and enter Northpark Wood. Continue with the Coldwaltham road and later recross the River Arun at Greatham Bridge. On reaching Coldwaltham turn left on to the A29 Bognor Regis road. Shortly pass through Watersfield and in ½ mile turn right on to the B2138 (signed Petworth), then almost immediately turn left on to the unclassified West Burton/Bignor road. Half a mile farther turn left and continue to West Burton (see page 67). Here turn right, signed Roman Villa and Bignor. After a mile pass the entrance to Bignor Roman Villa and Museum (right).

At the edge of Bignor village (see page 36) bear right, then at the church turn right, signed Sutton. Proceed to Sutton where the drive again turns right, signed Petworth. In 1¼ miles at the crossroads turn left. Shortly pass the attractive Burton water-mill and pond. Here stoneground flour is for sale, and the process by which it is made seen.

One mile farther turn right on to the A285 and later cross the River Rother before reaching the outskirts of Petworth (see page 58). This medieval town of narrow winding streets crowds up to the walls of Petworth House (NT) – a large late 17th- to 19th-century mansion situated in a great park.

The main drive turns left on to the A272 Midhurst road, (for the town centre keep forward). Continue through Tillington and later enjoy a delightful stretch in Cowdray Park before Easebourne. Here bear left and shortly recross the River Rother to enter Midhurst (see page 56). This is a pleasant town full of attractive houses and several fine old inns.

Follow Chichester signs to leave by the A286. Pass through Cocking (see page 40), then enter thickly-wooded downland en route to Singleton (see page 64). At the far end of the village turn left on to the unclassified Goodwood road. Almost immediately pass the Weald and Downland Open Air Museum on the right. (Alternatively remain on the A286 for a mile to visit the fine gardens at West Dean – see pages 27 and 70). The main tour ascends with extensive views to the left, passing beneath a hill called The Trundle (675ft). The grandstand of Goodwood Racecourse is then seen, and later the wooded grounds of Goodwood House are passed on the left (see page 49).

One mile beyond the entrance to the house turn right, signed Chichester. Half a mile farther at the roundabout junction with the bypass take the third exit on to the A285, and return to Chichester city centre.

Another section of the mosaic at Bignor, shown on page 36

Bishop's Palace, south-west of the cathedral in Chichester

PORTSMOUTH to	
Le Havre	5½ hrs
Guernsey	6½–7 hrs
St Malo	8½–10 hrs
Jersey	9–9½ hrs
Cherbourg	4–6½ hrs

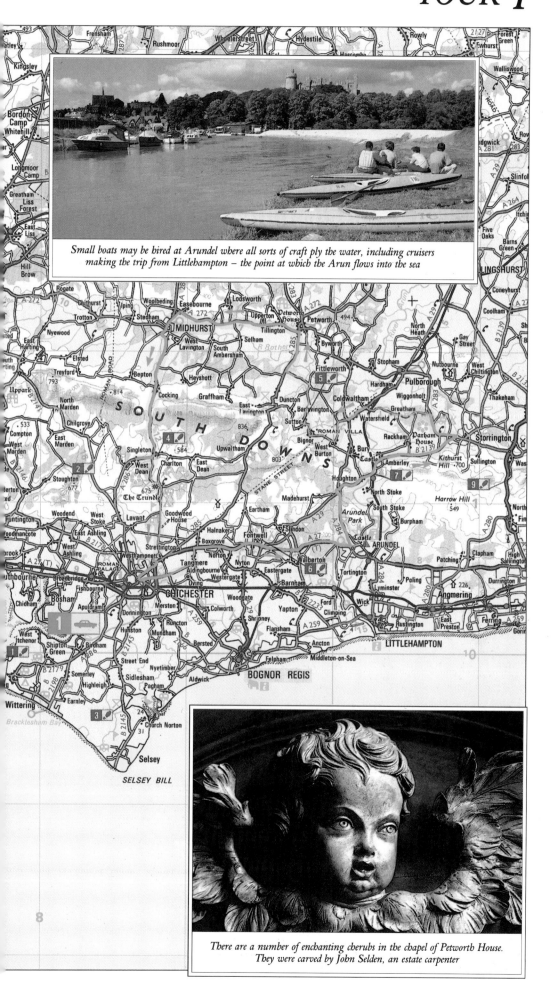

Small boats may be hired at Arundel where all sorts of craft ply the water, including cruisers making the trip from Littlehampton – the point at which the Arun flows into the sea

There are a number of enchanting cherubs in the chapel of Petworth House. They were carved by John Selden, an estate carpenter

TOUR 2

48 MILES

Across the Downs from Brighton

This drive takes in several attractive villages, the seaside resort of Seaford and the county town of East Sussex, Lewes. There are fine views of the Downs, the sea and the valleys of the Ouse and Cuckmere.

The drive starts from Brighton (see page 38), a town which in Regency times became the most fashionable resort in England, its centrepiece – then as now – the Royal Pavilion.

From Brighton follow signs to Lewes to leave by the A27. After 3 miles the drive leaves the built-up districts and passes Stanmer Park – the home of the University of Sussex. Here branch left on to the B2123, signed Falmer/Rottingdean, then at the roundabout turn right to cross the main road, still signed Rottingdean. An ascent is then made, crossing pleasant downland to reach a height of 536ft before descending past the residential area of Woodingdean into the attractive village of Rottingdean (see page 62). Here old buildings line the High Street and an early Georgian house contains the Grange Museum and Art Gallery.

At the far end turn left at the traffic-lights on to the A259 (no sign) and proceed with views of the chalk cliffs and the sea through Saltdean, Telscombe Cliffs and Peacehaven. After a short climb, later descend to the busy cross-channel port of Newhaven (see page 56) in the Ouse Valley. At the one-way system turn left then bear right, following the Seaford and Eastbourne signs. Of interest in the town is Fort Newhaven – a coastal artillery fort converted into a museum.

Cross the River Ouse and skirt Denton then Bishopstone before entering the residential town and resort of Seaford (see page 62). Follow the main A259 Eastbourne road through the town and in just over ¾ mile turn left on to an unclassified road, signed Alfriston. After a further 1½ miles there are fine views of the Cuckmere Valley from the High and Over Viewpoint (on the right). There is a steep descent of 1 in 5 followed by an ascent before reaching Alfriston (see page 32). This is considered to be one of the most attractive villages in Sussex, with several old buildings, notably the 13th-century Star Inn and the 14th-century Clergy House (NT).

At the market cross bear right and in 1¼ miles pass Drusilla's Zoo Park (on the right). At the next roundabout take the first exit to join the A27, signed Lewes, and follow the northern slopes of the Downs. Four miles farther a short detour can be made by turning left on to an unclassified road to visit the beautiful Georgian house of Firle Place (see page 46). This alternative can be extended by proceeding southwards to climb to the top of the Downs at 713ft near Firle Beacon.

The main tour continues along the A27 and in a mile it turns right, unclassified, signed Glynde and Ringmer. Shortly enter the village of Glynde (see page 49) and keep forward, passing the Elizabethan manor of Glynde Place on the right. In ¾ mile bear left, signed Ringmer. Pass the partly Tudor mansion of Glyndebourne – famous for its opera house (see page 60).

On reaching the junction with the B2192 turn left, signed Lewes. There are fine downland views on the left and across the Ouse Valley to the right before turning left after 1½ miles on to the A26 in order to visit Lewes – the county town of East Sussex (see page 52). Interesting features in the town include the Norman castle with its Barbican House Museum of Sussex Archaeology and the Museum of Local History in Anne of Cleves' House.

On entering the town keep forward at the mini-roundabouts (signed town centre) and cross the River Ouse. Turn left then right with the one-way system and ascend the main street. At the far end branch right, signed London/East Grinstead, then at the T-junction turn right again to leave by the A275. Later descend beneath the slopes of Offham Hill into Offham, then in ½ mile turn left on to the B2116, signed Hassocks. The route again follows the foot of the Downs to pass through Plumpton, famous for its racecourse, 1½ miles to the north.

Continue along the B2116 to Westmeston and here go forward with Underhill Road, unclassified (signed Narrow Lane). In ¾ mile turn left, signed The Beacon, and ascend a narrow winding road (1 in 10 gradient) to the summit of Ditchling Beacon. At 813ft it is one of the highest points on the South Downs and makes an excellent viewpoint.

Descend across undulating downland and in 2¼ miles pass a picnic site on the left. At the next T-junction turn left then turn right (no sign) and continue the descent to enter the suburbs of Brighton. After 3 miles turn left at the roundabout (signed town centre) then at traffic-lights turn right, A27, for the return to Brighton.

Lion at one of England's oldest inns – the Star at Alfriston

Beautiful stained glass by John Piper in St Peter's, Firle

Brighton's Palace Pier. Built in 1896–9, it stands near the site of the Old Chain Pier – the first pleasure pier to be built in England – which was swept away during a storm in 1896

TOUR 3 53 MILES
Inland from Beachy Head

From Beachy Head and the Seven Sisters, the drive passes one of England's smallest churches, an Augustinian Priory and the Royal Observatory at Herstmonceux to reach Pevensey, landing-place of William the Conqueror.

The drive starts from Eastbourne (see page 44), a popular holiday resort with an elegant Victorian and Edwardian sea front.

From the sea front follow the B2103 towards Beachy Head. After a winding ascent turn sharp left on to an unclassified road, signed Beachy Head. This road soon reaches the summit of Beachy Head.

Continue along the unclassified road past the disused Belle Tout Lighthouse to Birling Gap. Between here and Seaford are the chalk cliffs known as the Seven Sisters (NT).

The drive veers inland to East Dean (see page 44) where a left turn is made on to the A259 Seaford road. Ascend (1 in 6) to Friston (see page 48) and 2 miles farther descend (1 in 7) in to the valley of the Cuckmere River. At Exceat, at the foot of the hill, is the entrance to the Seven Sisters Country Park. Opposite is the fascinating Living World Museum of natural history (see page 44).

Take the next turning right on to an unclassified road, signed Litlington and Alfriston. In just over ¼ mile a short diversion to the right may be taken to the picturesque village of Westdean (see page 70).

The main drive continues along the winding road. A car park and forest walk are passed at the edge of Friston Forest on the right, and across the valley to the left a figure of a white horse cut into the hillside can be seen.

Proceed through Litlington and in ½ mile turn left, signed Alfriston. A detour (¼ mile) ahead leads to Lullington Church (see Alfriston, page 32), one of England's smallest churches at only 16ft square.

In ¾ mile bear left and cross the Cuckmere River then at the T-junction turn right, signed Berwick Station and Dicker. Alternatively turn left for Alfriston (see page 32). The main drive heads northwards and in ¼ mile passes the Drusilla's Zoo Park (on the right). At the next roundabout take the second exit and later go over the level crossing at Berwick Station. Two and a half miles farther the drive reaches Upper Dicker. Here a short detour to the right leads to Michelham Priory (see page 56), beside the Cuckmere River.

The main drive turns left, signed Golden Cross. In 1¼ miles turn left on to the A22 and nearly ½ mile farther take the next turning right, unclassified, signed Gun Hill. Continue with the Horam road and in 3¾ miles turn left on to the A267 and enter Horam. Branch right with the B2203, signed Heathfield, and proceed for 3 miles to the outskirts of Heathfield. At the junction with the A265 turn right, signed Hawkhurst, and follow a ridge of the Sussex Weald through Broad Oak, Burwash Weald and on to Burwash. Before entering this attractive village a turning to the right leads to Bateman's (NT), a 17th-century house and a former home of Rudyard Kipling.

In Burwash turn right on to an unclassified road, signed Wood's Corner. After crossing the River Dudwell gradually ascend and in 1 mile turn right. Continue the ascent, passing close to a gypsum mine (on the left), and near the 646ft summit go forward over the crossroads. Shortly at the T-junction turn right and then descend to Wood's Corner. At the Swan Inn turn right then immediately left, signed Bodle Street. In ¾ mile continue with the Ponts Green/Ashburnham road through pleasant countryside, then follow the Ninfield signs. Three miles farther at the junction with the B2204 turn right, signed Boreham Street. In another mile turn right again on to the A271 to reach Boreham Street. Half a mile beyond the village turn left, unclassified, signed Royal Greenwich Observatory and Pevensey. After another mile, on the right, is the entrance to Herstmonceux Castle; the partly-moated 15th-century building houses the Royal Greenwich Observatory (see page 51).

Continue to Wartling and at the Lamb Inn bear right, signed Pevensey (see page 59). The low-lying Pevensey Levels are then crossed to reach the edge of Pevensey – the Roman *Anderida*. William the Conqueror landed here in 1066 and the moated castle (AM) stands within Roman walls. There are several interesting buildings in the village, including the old Minthouse, built in 1342 and now a museum.

The main drive turns right on to the A259 then left at the traffic-lights, signed Pevensey Bay. Alternatively keep forward for the village and castle. At Pevensey Bay turn right for the return to Eastbourne.

Bateman's, an old ironmaster's house famous as Kipling's home

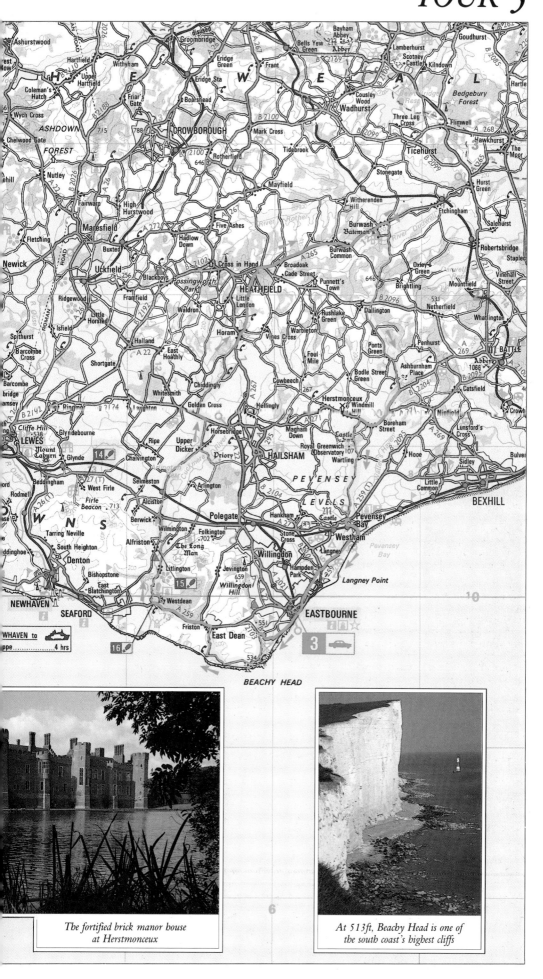

The fortified brick manor house
at Herstmonceux

At 513ft, Beachy Head is one of
the south coast's highest cliffs

WALK 1
East Head
Shoreline

Allow 1½ hours

Starting and finishing at West Wittering village, this shoreline walk offers good views of Chichester Harbour – and opportunities to swim – as it explores the dunes, margins and marshes of East Head (NT), before returning through Snow Hill Creek.

From West Wittering, follow signs to the car park and the sea, driving down a private road owned by West Wittering Estates to the car park (GR772979). Leave the car (fee charged) and walk down the road, through the car park, to the sea. A large notice board provided by the National Trust and the Chichester Harbour Conservancy gives information about the area.

Cross over the shingle bank, turn right and walk on the beach up the west side of East Head. This shingle and sand headland marks the eastern limit of the estuarine complex of Portsmouth, Langstone and Chichester Harbours. Left is Sandy Point – the

south-east tip of Hayling Island. These spits mark the entrance to Chichester Harbour, which was used by the Romans and continued to be of commercial importance well into the 19th century. Today, Chichester is one of the most popular recreational harbours in the country, and designated an area of outstanding natural beauty. East Head itself (NT) is constantly at risk from wind and tides, and has been in danger of disappearing. Thanks to the efforts of the Trust's volunteers, the erosion of the dunes has been arrested. To assist the Trust in this work, walkers are asked to avoid the fenced-off areas where marram grass growth is encouraged to stabilise the dunes. From the northern tip of East Head can be seen Bow Hill – on the Downs in the foreground – Thorney Island to the left and Goodwood to the right. On a clear day it is even possible to glimpse the spire of Chichester Cathedral.

Complete the circuit of the headland, keeping close to the dunes on the east side and avoiding wandering into the salt marsh. Avoid the footpath back into the car park, bearing left instead to follow a path along the shore towards the pink house within sight at Snow Hill Creek. After a rest on the green at Snow Hill Creek, leave the shore path and turn right through a metal gate, following the footpath along a private road. Cross another road and carry straight on towards the church. Emerge on to a public road beside a pair of brick-and-flint cottages, turn right and visit West Wittering parish church. Dedicated to St Peter and St Paul, the church dates from Norman times and contains some interesting monuments.

Continue past the village school to a junction with the private road which leads back to the car park. Turn right here, and walk on the footpath beside the road back to the car. There is safe bathing from the beach by the car park.

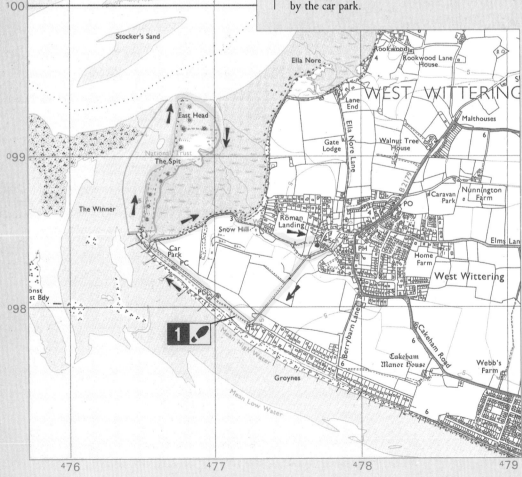

Jays are woodland members of the crow family

Wildham Wood

Allow 1¾ hours

A flavour of the wooded western Downs and a visit to the remote village of East Marden are features of this walk, which follows a circular route through Forestry Commission broad-leaved woodland.

Park in the Forestry Commission car park below Stoughton Down, about a mile north east of Stoughton village (GR815126). Walk up the road towards East Marden and after 200–300yds turn right and follow a footpath along the southern edge of Wildham Wood, refusing an early opportunity to turn left into the interior. Commercial forestry is an important economic activity on the Downs and is well demonstrated at Wildham, which is of planted beech ranging between 25 and 40 years old. Most of the plantation occupies an ancient woodland site that was formerly managed with oak and ash standards over an understorey of hazel. Beech woodland under the control of the Forestry Commission in the area covers some 1,000 acres.

As it climbs towards East Marden Down, largely following the edge of the wood, the path becomes steeper, affording views back over the wooded western downland. Just past Hillbarn, turn left along a footpath between a field and a copse, climb a stile and follow the path down a steep hillside. A rest on the short downland turf offers the opportunity to enjoy views to East Marden, with its red-roofed cottages, on the far side of the valley.

Press on towards the village, following the path through a farmyard, and join a road by Postman's Cottage. Here turn left and visit the church and the much-photographed village well. Bear in mind the advice of E V Lucas: 'East Marden, however, has no inn and is therefore not the best friend of the traveller'.

Retrace the route to the farmyard and take the path due south between the hay-barn and the stockyard. Climb a stile into the following field, walk south to another stile on the right, cross this into the adjacent field and continue straight on (south), keeping the hedge to the left. Finally, cross an open field to reach the road by a large beech tree. Cross the road and take the path opposite to continue straight on into the wood, climbing. At the top of the hill, after a large field opens out on the right, turn left at a junction to continue along a bridleway which follows a broad ride through the woodland. Ignore all paths to the right and left, descending through the wood to a road by Wildham Barn, and a brick-and-flint house with pretty Victorian gables. Turn right and walk back along the road to the car park.

WALK 3
Pagham Harbour

Allow 2 hours

Sections of the path followed by this route through the 1,000-acre maritime nature reserve of Pagham Harbour flood at or near high tide. *Tide tables – such as those in the AA Members' Handbook – should be consulted before any outing.* A pair of binoculars and a visit to the local information centre beforehand will add greatly to the pleasure of the walk.

Start in the Pagham Harbour nature-reserve car park, and from the information centre at Sidlesham ferry (GR856967) follow a surfaced path signed Pagham Harbour and Sidlesham Mill. Go through the gate at the end of the path and turn left, following the old tramway route from Chichester to Selsey. Meet a road, turn right and walk to the quay. This is still accessible by boat at high tide, although landing is now controlled in the interests of nature conservation.

Take the shoreline footpath to the right of the brick and sandstone garage, noting a warning that the path floods at high tide. Keeping the hedge and wall close to the left, follow the path round the harbour on to Pagham Wall. An opportunity now presents itself to observe seabirds and wildfowl at close quarters.

Huge flocks of redshanks congregate on the coast in winter

On Pagham Wall, almost due south of Honer Farm, turn left off the coastal path and take a footpath north into a field. At the top of the field, follow a footpath left before reaching the farm, climb over a stile, then cross a field and enter a wood. Cross a footbridge and continue west (straight on) along the path across an open field. Continue with a footpath sign, climb a gate and join a grassy track past a barn on the left, with Marsh Farm away to the right. After the barn, the track becomes a concrete road. Follow this for about 150yds and turn left into a field.

Continue along a path south, negotiate New Barn and reach a road. Cross over and pick up the path almost immediately opposite. Follow the path as it bears left beside a wall, and eventually emerge on to the road by Old Mill Farm. Turn right and walk along the road for about 200yds to the junction with the tramway path from the information centre. Turn left on to the path and follow it back to the car park.

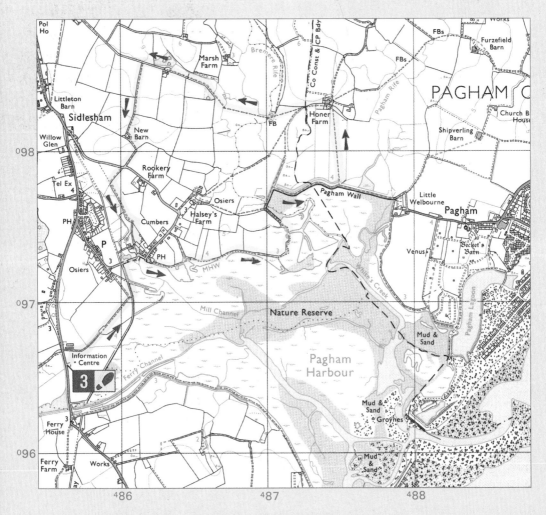

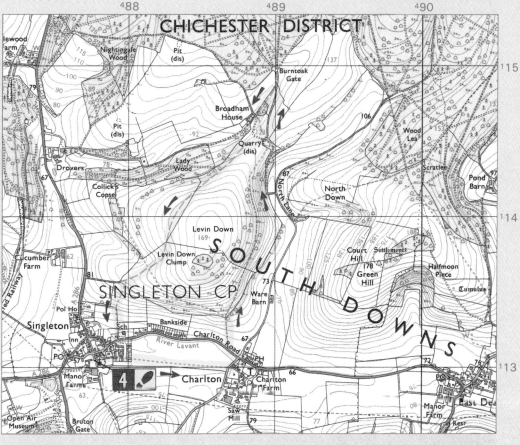

Downland Chase

Allow 1¼ hours

Splendid downland is a major attraction of this walk, which explores famous hunting and racing country while affording views across the valley of the Lavant to Goodwood and The Trundle.

Park near Singleton church (GR878131). Once owned by Earl Godwin, father of King Harold, Singleton came to more recent prominence when Goodwood race-course was opened in 1801. In 1880 the railway arrived and a fine station (now a winery) was built between Singleton and West Dean. Visited on more than one occasion by royalty, the village continues to attract trippers with the superb Weald and Downland Museum.

Take the footpath east from the churchyard, pass through modern housing and cross open fields to the Charlton Estate, through which flows the Lavant chalk stream – though not always in summer, since it is a 'winterbourne'. In the 18th century Charlton was renowned as the home of the most famous hunt in England, with more than 150 horses stabled there at one time. Its crowning glory was a 10-hour chase in 1738, which ended at Arundel Park.

Reach the road in Charlton and turn left, then at the main road, turn left again. After 100yds take a steep path right on to Levin Down. Climb a stile, then in a short while another, and ascend the eastern face of the Down, forking left in a few yards.

After some time, as the chalk track comes into sight

Numerous bridleways open up the Downs to horse riders

in the valley below, bear right into a wood, following the footpath. When the path emerges from the wood, continue beside an open field. Keep the Old Charlton Hunt waypost to the left and walk straight ahead (north) following the bridleway. At the T-junction, before the bridleway enters Singleton Forest, turn sharp left to Broadham House. Go through the field gate by the farm and turn left up the chalky track. At the waypost, go through a bridlegate and turn left, then pass through the field gate past a 'Boundary of Open Country' sign. These signs show that public access to Levin Down is by agreement between the landowner and the county council.

Walk over the Down in a generally south-westerly (diagonally-right) direction. At the top, go through a field gate and make for a signpost on open downland, then head in the same direction to another signpost. Views south encompass Goodwood race-course, The Trundle (with its radio masts), Singleton village and the buildings of the open-air museum.

Go left over the stile above the school, then descend to the village and car park. Leave time to visit the two pleasant village inns and – in summer – to watch cricket on the green.

WALK 5

Bignor and Beech Hangers

Allow 2½ hours

A strenuous climb up Bignor Hill (NT) – in an area well known for its superb Roman relics – is rewarded by a gentler stroll along the escarpment and an easy descent to the downland villages of Barlavington and Sutton.

Park in Sutton village, near the White Horse (GR978153). Take the path to the right of a thatched cottage opposite the pub, and cross the field. Cross a stream by two footbridges and climb along its bank through woods to a road. Turn right, and just past Malthouse Cottages take a footpath to the right – then turn almost immediately left. At the next junction, bear left along the hedge line and, following the path, ascend the hill. Reach a stile at the fringe of the wood, cross a track and pick up the path again on the other side – slightly to the right. Climb steeply through the woods in a diagonally-right direction and meet the road. Turn right and walk up the road to a waypost by the

National Trust car park, at the top of Bignor Hill. The waypost points out the route of the Roman Stane Street, which ran from the East Gate of Chichester to Billingsgate in London and was built in about AD70. Just off the route at Bignor is the famous villa, which is well worth a visit. One of the excavated rooms is now used as a museum, and items found on the site include animal skulls and bones. A model indicates how the villa might have looked.

From the car park, take a chalky track past the National Trust 'no cars' sign, cross Stane Street on its embankment and continue with radio masts to the left. Keep straight on where a bridleway joins from the left and walk down the hill. After about ½ mile turn right on to a signposted bridleway through woodland. After about 30yds, where the path divides into three, take the extreme left-hand fork and follow it generally straight on between two fields. Go through the gate and follow the track uphill among beech woods. Cross a bridle gate at the top and descend over an open field. At the bottom of the field cross a track, ignore the first path to the right into the woods and take the second, a few yards farther on. This descends to Barlavington. Follow the path to the road and walk up the no-through road to Barlavington church.

Pass through the churchyard and along a farm track, then turn right by a row of trees and walk towards Sutton church. Turn right over a stile into a field, cross the stream, climb through woodland and out into the field. Keeping the hedge line to the left, take the bridleway left to Sutton at the T-junction. Join the village street by the church, turn right and walk back to the White Horse and the car.

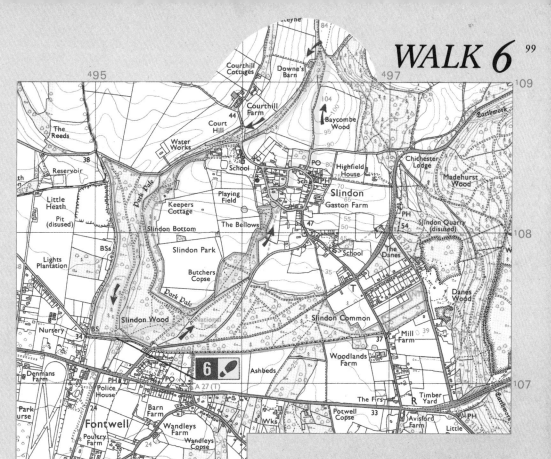

Slindon Woods

Allow 1½ hours

Easy and level, this walk explores picturesque Slindon village (NT) and the famous natural and man-made attractions of the Slindon Estate – including ancient beech woods and the largest surviving section of the Roman Stane Street.

Park in the National Trust Slindon Beech Woods car park, just north of Fontwell (GR952073), and leave by a gate into the woods. Take the path which forks right, continue past a track on the left, join a metalled path and turn left. Cross a track and eventually reach a pair of gates. Go straight ahead, bear left to join a path from the right and keep right at a tree in the middle of the path. Emerge on to the road by Slindon village pond. The National Trust owns the 3,500-acre Slindon Estate, which includes much of the 17th-century brick-and-flint village and extends to the escarpment of the Downs at Bignor Hill. Features include the largest surviving section (3½ miles) of Stane Street and a shingle beach that was left as the sea withdrew from the area, centuries past.

Turn left and walk up the road, turn right into Dyers Lane and then right at the T-junction by Hill House. Take the first turning left by Mill Lane House, or carry straight on to visit the Newburgh Arms. Go up the lane beside Mill Lane House and continue straight on along a bridleway at a point where the lane bends right. Follow the bridleway to the end of the wood and then take a 'U' turn left to Downe's Barn. Follow the bridleway south-west, diverting – if the track is too muddy – on to the parallel permissive footpath at the National Trust 'no horses' sign. Emerge on the road opposite the entrance to Slindon College and turn right, following the road for about 200yds. Turn left at the National Trust sign into Slindon Woods and follow the track round to the right. Pass Keeper's Cottage, take the right fork and after 200–300yds take the path forking down to the right. Keep straight on in a generally southerly direction to rejoin the car park.

Beeches can grow to 150ft high and live for 200 years

WALK 7
Amberley Mount

Allow 2½ hours

During a long and easy ascent through open agricultural land towards the beech clump crowning Rackham Hill, this route affords good views across the meandering River Arun before veering off to cross Amberley Mount on the South Downs Way.

Park in Amberley station car park by the entrance to the Chalk Pits Museum (GR026118). This fascinating museum of the industrial history of southern England is well worth a visit. Opened in 1979, it received a regional award from the Automobile Association in 1987 and has many exciting developments planned. At least two hours should be allowed to do it justice. Refreshments are available.

Walk down to the road, turn left and walk under the railway bridge. Turn left again after the bridge, pass the Bridge Inn and walk down a lane to North Stoke. At the T-junction by the telephone box, turn right to visit North Stoke church. Domesday recorded a church at North Stoke in 1087, but there is nothing in the present building earlier than the 13th century. The windows in both transepts are some of the best examples of early tracery in southern England and there is a crude sundial scratched fairly high up on the outside wall of the south transept.

Retrace the route to the telephone box and junction, then continue straight up the road in a gentle ascent. Spectacular views of the Arun Valley open out to the right with the 'Alpine' spire of the church at South Stoke on the other side of the river. Beyond is Arundel Park, and in good weather it is possible to glimpse a distant view of the distinctive outline of Arundel Castle.

After a very long but quite easy climb, pass Canada Barn on the right and bear left, following the road as it degenerates into a farm track. Carry straight on at the path crossroads towards the top of the hill, turn left at the next junction and head up the hill with a stand of trees ahead known as Rackham Clump – once the home of Sussex charcoal-burners. *At the next junction turn left and follow a bridleway to its junction with the South Downs Way. Here turn left again and follow the Way to Amberley Mount.* To the north, the River Arun can be seen meandering its way towards the sea through the low-lying Amberley Wild Brooks and the Amberley Gap. Amberley village – with its castle (once the summer home of the Bishops of Chichester), church and thatched cottages – can be seen far below.

Descend Amberley Mount and – keeping alongside the fence to the right and ignoring all left turns – continue with Downs Farm to the left. Walk on past Highdown and along the surfaced road of High Titten, peering down into the Chalk Pits Museum in the quarry to the left. Join the very busy main road at the bottom and, exercising great care, turn left and return to the station car park.

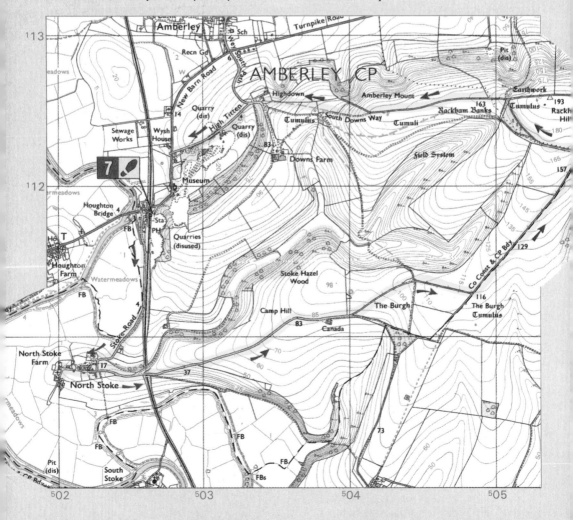

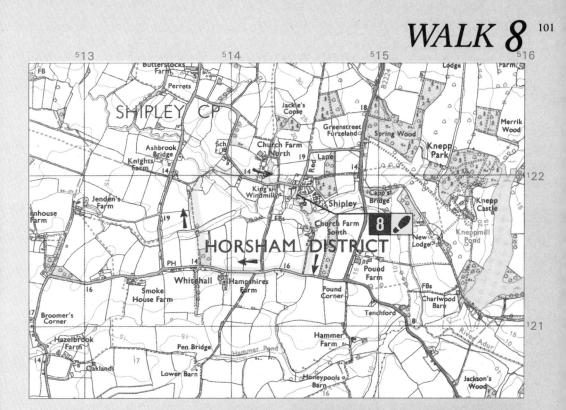

Shipley Windmill

Allow 1½ hours

This short, level stroll around the charming Wealden village of Shipley – particularly suitable for older and younger members of the family – includes a visit to the famous working smock-mill once owned by writer Hilaire Belloc, now restored in his memory.

Park in Shipley near the parish church (GR145218) of St Mary the Virgin. This was originally built for the Knights Templar in the 12th century, and on the right-hand wall of the nave has a memorial stone to John Ireland, the composer and church musician.

Shipley, hidden some five miles from Horsham, means 'the place of the sheep pasture' and the village consists of a couple of farms, a school and a few cottages and houses. Hilaire Belloc, the writer and traveller, lived here from 1906 to 1953. His house, King's Land, is a fine old Wealden house with a Horsham-slab roof on the western edge of the village. In the grounds stands Shipley windmill, built in 1879 and now the best surviving working smock mill in Sussex. It is a wooden structure standing on a brick base and the cap on the top can be adjusted to turn the sweeps into the wind. Belloc loved Sussex and his enthusiasm is best conveyed in his poem *The South Country*:

> *The great hills of the South Country*
> *They stand along the sea;*
> *And it's there walking in the high woods*
> *That I could wish to be.*

Today, Belloc is perhaps best remembered for his light verse, including his *Cautionary Tales for Children*.

After visiting the church, follow the path opposite the south door to enter a field through a kissing-gate. A

Anglo-French writer Hilaire Belloc lived in Sussex

stream which eventually becomes the mighty River Adur flows through the field on its way to the sea at Shoreham.

Bear left, following the signpost direction, then cross the field to a footbridge by Church Farm South. Cross the bridge, then continue along a track between the farm buildings. Turn right when the path meets the road and walk on the grass verge for about 400yds. Leave the road and turn right on a footpath just past Hampshire Cottage – or continue along the road for another 200yds to The Countryman inn. Follow the path along the right-hand edge of the field and climb over the stile into a wood. Cross a footbridge over the stream and follow the path round the western edge of the field.

Climb a stile to the right of the tile-and-wood Sussex barn, then join a bridleway at a T-junction and turn right. Cross the stream and follow the bridleway through a field gate. Head for the corner of the field in the direction of the windmill, go through a wicket gate, join the road and turn right. Walk back to the village past Church Farm North, King's Land and the 19th-century windmill. From the windmill are views of Chanctonbury Ring and the Downs. Maintained by a charitable trust, it is open often.

WALK 9
Chanctonbury Ring

Allow 2½ hours

**Views from prehistoric Chanctonbury Ring are
well worth the steep climb necessary to reach it.
The going is easier on the descent through
beech woods to the village of Washington –
whose inn, according to writer Hilaire Belloc,
served the very best beer in Sussex. Parts of the
route can be very muddy.**

*Turn east off the A24 at Highden Hill, between
Washington and Findon, and drive up the access track
to Washington Lime Quarry. Before the quarry
entrance, bear right to a small car park provided by the
County Council (GR121119). Following South Downs
Way signposts, climb a track to the 750ft hilltop and
turn left towards Chanctonbury Ring.* Before going
on, pause to look at the dewpond on the left of the
path, originally constructed in 1870 and restored
by the Society of Sussex Downsmen. Dewponds,
built to provide drinking water for cattle and sheep
on the Downs, were lined with puddled clay to
retain rain-water. Sometimes they were built on a
slope, in which case the down-hill side always
features distinctive banking.

Walk on to Chanctonbury Ring. Strictly speaking,
the 'Ring' is an Iron Age hillfort, and not the
clump of beech trees which crowns its hilltop site
and has become a landmark throughout the
western Downs. The clump was planted by a
member of the Goring family of Wiston House,
who organised the project when a boy and lived to
see the trees reach maturity. There are good views

*Shepherds who looked after the huge flocks of sheep that
grazed the Downs lived hard and lonely lives, and were
often on the hills for weeks on end*

in all directions from the Ring, extending as far as
Cissbury in the south east.

*Continue on the South Downs Way to a junction.
Turn sharp left, leaving the Way, and follow the path
downhill through Chalkpit Wood. At the bottom of the
hill turn left on a bridleway, past a brick-and-flint
cottage. Walk on past Owlscroft Barn, through the
northern fringe of the wood and eventually emerge at a
footpath crossroads. Here go straight ahead across two
open fields, then follow the path along a hedge line, past
Tilley's Farm to the road. Turn right to visit the
Franklands Arms, then walk back up the road to the
quarry access track and car park.* On the way is an
opportunity to turn off the road and walk down
The Street to Washington church, which is worth
a visit (allow extra time for this). E V Lucas
concluded that there are few better spots in the
country than Washington for a modest contented
man to live and keep a horse. 'Rents are low,
turfed hills are near, and there is good hunting.'

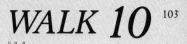

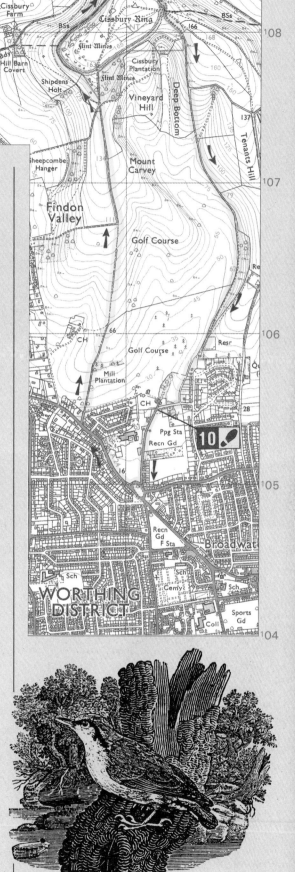

Cissbury Ring

Allow 2½ hours

Clearly visible from its neighbour Chanctonbury Ring, Cissbury is the most impressive Iron Age hillfort in Sussex and is enjoyed all the more during an expedition which also takes in other features of the fine downland rising up behind Worthing.

Leave the A27 at the Broadwater roundabout, north of Worthing, turning into Hillbarn Lane – signed Hill Barn Golf Course. Drive down Hillbarn Lane, past the Excess Insurance Group building, and park in the public car park at the far end of the recreation ground (GR143055). Walk back along Hillbarn Lane to the A24, turn right and continue beside the main road for about 300yds, then turn right up a bridleway. Walk straight up the bridleway towards the Downs for about half an hour, with the golf course mainly to the right. At the top, where a footpath joins from the left, go through the bridlegate and pause to take in the view. Ahead loom the ramparts of Cissbury Ring, to the right is an old beech wood and beyond lie Vineyard Hill and Deep Bottom. Left is the urban sprawl of the Findon Valley.

Bear centre-left across the grass to a fence stile, climb over and follow the path up steps to the top of the rampart. Bear left and follow the path around the monument. The massive ditch and rampart, a mile long, enclose a 60-acre site which commands the surrounding landscape. Fortified by Iron Age man as a defensive position protecting a very large area, the site was the most important in Sussex and in scale surpassed others at The Trundle and Whitehawk. It fell into disuse under the Romans, but was re-fortified by the Saxons. Known simply as 'Bury' until the 18th century from the old English 'burh', a defended position, the addition of the prefix reflects a supposed association with the Saxon Cissa, Lord of Chichester. From the northern rampart are good views north to Chanctonbury and east to Truleigh Hill and Newtimber Hill.

Continue over sheep-cropped turf to the north-eastern portal of the monument, at which point leave through a gate and bear right to head south-east along a grassy track to a bridlepath signpost. Go straight ahead through a gate and follow the bridleway south along the eastern edge of a golf course. After a while pass a brick-and-flint barn, then houses and gardens on the left. Reach a T-junction and turn right on to a metalled road, past a waterworks. The car park is at the end of the road on the left.

Nuthatches, which are found in woodland, parks and gardens, can hop up and down the trunks of trees

SCALE 1:25 000

WALK 11

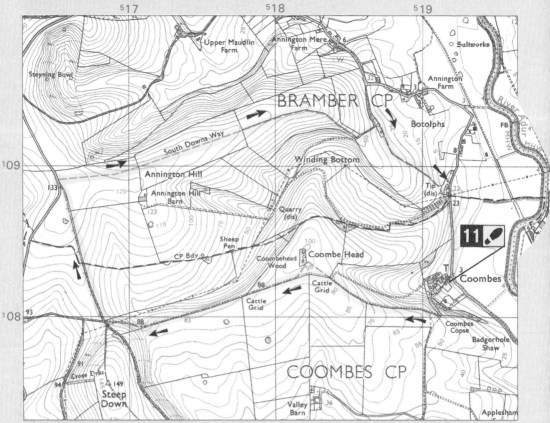

Sea Views from Annington Hill

Allow 2 hours

This visit to the downland settlement of Coombes includes a bracing but fairly gentle walk around Annington Hill, with good views to the sea and across the Adur Valley. Coombes church is delightful.

The rare woodlark is recognised by its haunting song

From the A27, turn north on the west side of the Adur bridge – beneath Lancing College – and drive up a narrow lane to the hamlet of Coombes. Turn off the road and park by the telephone box below Coombes church and Church Farm (GR192082). Walk up the footpath to the church, go through the churchyard and continue up through a copse to a footpath junction. Here turn right, go through a gate and turn immediately left to follow a fence across the hillside towards Coombehead Wood, with a good view of Coombes down to the right. Cross the cattle grid and follow the bridleway along a farm track towards Steep Down. Eventually, after another cattle grid, leave the track where it bears right and head left under an electricity power line. Climb up the field to a footpath signpost distantly visible on the skyline. At that junction turn right and follow a broad, grassy green-lane for some distance. Emerge at a road, turn right and after 100yds turn right again on to the South Downs Way.

Follow the Way for about a mile, with views north

to Steyning and Bramber – and east to Truleigh Hill and the Upper Beeding cement works. Pass Bramber Beeches. These trees were planted by the county federation of Women's Institutes to mark their jubilee. From the top of the hill are views of Lancing College, with its prominent chapel.

After climbing the hill, reach a junction and turn left along the South Downs Way, then descend past farm buildings to the entrance of Tin Pots Cottage. Here, where the track bears left, almost immediately leave the South Downs Way on a bridleway to the right, through a narrow belt of trees. Emerge from the trees and turn immediately right, passing the cottage and keeping close to the wood. Follow the path to the right of a disused tip, climb through scrub and turn left at the top of the hill, by the pylon. At the road turn right and walk the short distance back along it to the car.

Church Farm, Coombes, welcomes visits by school parties and organised groups, who are taken on guided tours of the farm by Jenny Passmore, the farmer's daughter. Enquiries by post, or telephone Shoreham-by-Sea (0273) 452028.

Devil's Dyke

Allow 2½ hours minimum

Starting at Devil's Dyke, this route drops down to villages nestling along the springline at the foot of the Downs, then regains the summits after a stiff hillside climb.

Park at the Devil's Dyke Hotel (GR258111). The view north extends over the Weald, and to the west takes in the beech clump of Chanctonbury Ring.

Leave the car park, walk back along the road and turn left along the South Downs Way. Look down into the steep dry valley, created it is said by the devil to flood the Christian communities of the Weald. Happily, his work was not completed.

Following the Way, walk over Summer Down to the main road, opposite Saddlescombe Farm. Ahead is Newtimber Hill, with its old chalk quarry. The farm is noted for its well-house, which has a donkey-driven winding wheel and is the subject of the charming memoir of 19th-century downland life, *A South Down Farm in the Sixties.*

Take the path into the field on the left and walk round the wood. Follow the rather obscure signpost, keep to the right of the field, descend into a muddy hollow and cross the stile. Turn right down the path, then very soon leave the path by crossing a stile on the left into another field, keeping a stream on the right. Climb the grassy bank, keeping close to the right of the field, and

enjoy rolling meadow-land on the way to Poynings, emerging on the road via a stile. It is possible that temporary fencing may restrict this section. Turn right up the road to visit Poynings church. Here, take in the interesting display about Dr Samuel Holland who – somewhat to his surprise – found himself Rector there in the 19th century.

Return and take the path on the right, off the road, passing through a gate into the field. Keep to the right of the field, through an iron gate, and bear right following a close-boarded fence where the paths converge. Go through a wicket gate, cross the stream footbridge and turn left at the signpost to follow a surfaced twitten to its junction with Mill Lane. Turn left and follow a concrete road beside the stream.

Pass a sewage works, a ruined brick-and-flint farmstead and a small dam, then leave the stream at a wooden footbridge and follow the path over a field, through an iron gate, over a stile and into a big, open field. Keeping Chanctonbury ahead to the left, arrive eventually at a road. Turn right and walk past a house with a tennis court. Cross the stream and turn left on to the footpath by Brookside Liveries. Follow the path by the stream, cross the bridge and head south towards Fulking. At the corner of the field turn right over a stile, and after 100yds turn left round the edge of the field. On the far side, cross a stile over a post-and-rail fence. Join the road and turn right to the Shepherd and Dog. Walk across the pub car park (under the trellis) and follow the public path, then turn right and begin the climb up to the Dyke Hotel. Ascend steps and head for the prominent signpost on the skyline, then continue straight up the chalky track to the summit. Go through the gate and follow the path along the crest of the hill to the hotel.

WALK *13*

Ditchling Beacon

Allow 2½ hours

This is a walk of contrasts, encompassing the bracing escarpment of the Downs above Ditchling and the sheltered valleys of the dip slope, falling gently away to the sea.

From the A273 near Clayton turn into Mill Lane and drive up the hill to the public car park beside Jill Mill (GR303135). Jack and Jill are famous Sussex landmarks. Jack is the taller mill, built in 1876; Jill was dragged there by oxen from Brighton in the 1850s. The village of Clayton, at the bottom of the hill, has a parish church with interesting wall paintings.

Walk up the track, past Jack Mill, and turn left at the junction with the South Downs Way, where there is a stone bridleway marker. Walk along the Way for nearly 2 miles to Ditchling Beacon car park, ignoring all paths to the right. On the way pass Keymer Post, which marks the boundary between West and East Sussex, and look out for dewponds – constructed by farmers to provide drinking water for their

sheep. Enjoy views to the north over the Weald and note the fine downland turf, particularly in the area managed as a nature reserve. At 813ft, Ditchling Beacon (NT) is the third highest point on the Sussex Downs and is the site of an Iron Age hillfort. It was also part of a chain of summits on which beacon fires were lit to warn of the Spanish Armada. This now belongs to the National Trust, to whom it was given in memory of a pilot killed in the Battle of Britain in August 1940.

Return from Ditchling Beacon car park along the main track, passing first a triangulation point and then a scrub-filled dewpond on the left. At the old pond turn left on to a gated bridleway and follow it between large flinty fields. This is a good place to see flints, the irregular stones composed almost entirely of silica which occur in the chalk and have been used by man since earliest times for tools and weapons.

Keep straight on through double gates, and where another gated bridleway joins from the left, then descend steeply to a metal field gate and bear diagonally right, signposted Lower Standean. Follow the centre of a sheltered valley, winding right and leaving the field through a metal gate.

Continue along the valley, or combe, and where it swings left go through a wooden gate with a blue waymark and turn sharp left to follow the fence. Ascend a chalky path and cross a ridge to Lower Standean Farm. At the bridleway junction, turn right, signed Keymer Post. Pass brick-and-flint buildings on the left, ignore a left turn and follow the track through a bedgeline. Climb up out of the valley, following the bridleway signposts and at the crossroads turn right through a hedge boundary and continue across open fields. Soon, Jack Mill can be seen ahead to the left, with Woolstonbury Hill behind. Rejoin the South Downs Way at Keymer Post, turn left and walk to car park.

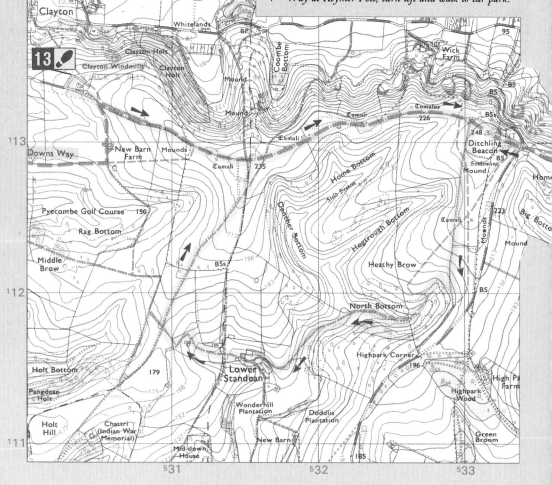

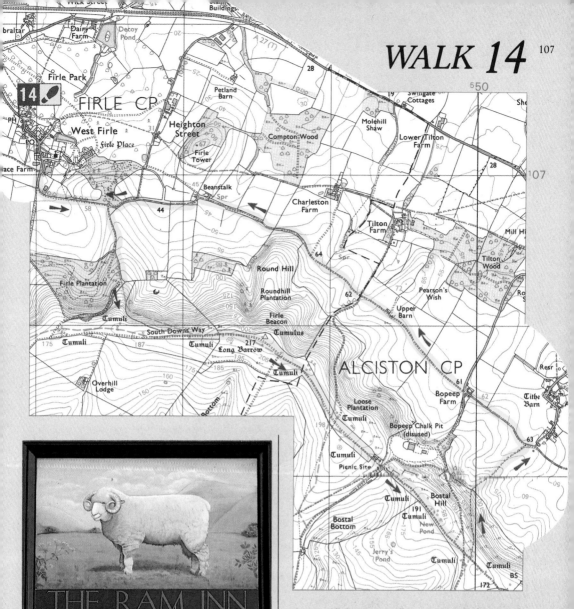

Because this Southdown ram looked odd without horns, the pub-sign artist gave it some from a Dorset breed

Firle Beacon

Allow 3 hours

This walk from Firle village involves an exhilarating climb to Firle Beacon, a rolling walk on the top of the Downs – with fine views in all directions – and a level stroll along an old coach road back to the village.

Turn off the A27 east of Lewes, signposted Firle. Drive into the village and park near The Ram Inn (GR468074). This is named after the crest of the Gage family of Firle Place. Firle is a particularly attractive and unspoilt downland village which grew up around Firle Place and the parish church of St Peter. The Gage family remained Catholics until well into the 18th century and Firle was held for the King during the Civil War when neighbouring Glynde was a Parliamentary stronghold under Colonel Morley. Sir John Gage and his wife, Philippa, are the subjects of the quite beautiful alabaster effigies in the church, and there are a number of very good brasses which can be rubbed

for a small fee. An excellent note on the history of Firle by Viscount Gage is on sale in the church.

From The Ram, walk down the village street and along the bridleway through Place Farm towards the Downs. Follow the path left along the field edge, then at the junction turn right and climb up the side of the field and a copse towards the top, looking back to admire Firle Tower on its hill. Join the South Downs Way at the summit, turn left and walk along the escarpment for about 2 miles. Walk past Firle Beacon triangulation point, at over 700ft, and the car park at the top of Bo-Peep bostal. Bostal is the Sussex term for a road or track which ascends the scarp of the Downs. Enjoy the views south to Newhaven, Cuckmere Haven and the Seven Sisters.

Climb Bostal Hill and, just over the brow, bear left across open downland to a stile in the fence. Climb the stile and follow the path down the hill, over another stile and through hedgerow woodland. As the tithe barn at Alciston comes into view, turn left along an old coach road, following it for about 2 miles to Firle. Be careful not to go straight on towards the tithe barn. The coach road under the Downs carried all traffic until 1812, and its often muddy condition gives a good idea of travel problems in days gone by.

Walk past Bo-Peep Farm, Upper Barn and the old Beanstalk – formerly an inn on the coach road and now a pair of cottages – below Firle Tower. Bear left and then right at the Beanstalk, and follow the track straight on to the village and the car. Allow time to explore the village, where there are cast-iron house numbers and a particularly fine house hung with mathematical tiles, designed to look like bricks.

WALK 15
The Long Man

Allow 2½ hours

Partly on the high, bare downland of East Sussex and partly in one of the county's rare areas of undisturbed heath, this walk visits the curious Long Man of Wilmington chalk figure after exploring the exquisite little village of Alfriston, on the Cuckmere.

Park by the church at Alfriston (GR522030). The 'Cathedral of the South Downs' is an appropriate focal point for this exceptionally pretty – if popular – riverside village, known for its inns and tea gardens. Next to the church is the Clergy House, which was the first property to be acquired by the National Trust.

Cross the River Cuckmere by the white bridle-bridge near the church and follow a metalled path to the road. Cross the road by Plonk Barn and take the footpath signed Lullington Church. Continue to the church, ignoring a sign to the South Downs Way. Lullington is the smallest church in Sussex, being only the chancel of a once larger building. There is a solitary grave in the churchyard.

Return to the brick path and continue left to the road. Turn left and follow the road for about 400yds to the hill crest, then turn right and join the South Downs Way. Towards the top of the hill keep straight on, even though the South Downs Way bears right, and follow the fence line. Below, on the north face of the hill, is the Long Man of Wilmington – a figure 240ft high, outlined originally in chalk. His origins are obscure, one story being that he was cut by the monks of the Benedictine priory at Wilmington – the ruins of which can be seen adjoining the farmhouse in the valley below.

Keep straight on beside the fence to a gate, then bear right alongside another fence to rejoin the South Downs

Banded snails are among many that favour dry downland

Way through a bridlegate in about 20yds. Follow the Way partly round the rim of a deep combe for about 300yds, then strike off diagonally left to pick up a concrete South Downs Way marker. Continue to a second marker, then uphill over open downland to a fence. Follow the fence right, then near a roofless barn continue right past a wood to crossroads. Turn right, leaving the South Downs Way, and walk through the edge of Lullington Heath National Nature Reserve – an unusual example of chalk heathland – following signs to Litlington. Avoid the path left into the nature reserve, signed Charleston Bottom. At the next junction, as views of Alfriston and the Cuckmere Valley open up, bear right on a path signed Lullington Court. Join the road at Lullington Court, turn right and then left, signed Alfriston. Walk along the road to Plonk Barn, turn left and follow the path back to the village.

Seven Chalk Cliffs

Allow 3 hours

Exploring perhaps the most famous section of
downland in Sussex, this classic route visits
Friston Forest, the chalk cliffs of the Seven
Sisters, the estuary of Cuckmere Haven and the
meanders of the Cuckmere Valley.

*Park in the public car park south of the A259, at the
excellent Seven Sisters Country Park Centre at Exceat
(GR518995). Cross the road with care and follow
South Down Way signs up the hill to the right of the
centre. Climb over the flint wall at the top and go
straight on, soon climbing down a stepped slope through
woodland to Westdean village. Turn right by the pond,
signed Friston and Jevington. Follow the road and –
where it curves left – continue straight on into Friston
Forest.*

*After a pair of white cottages and a vineyard, bear
right up a chalky track signed Friston. Follow the broad
forest ride for about half an hour, ignoring all paths to
the right and left. Eventually, reach a road opposite a
brick-and-flint barn, and turn left, signed Friston.
Follow this uphill to a gate and stay with it as it
swings sharply downhill to the right. Half way up the
subsequent rise turn right over a stile into a field, signed
Friston and East Dean. Cross the field to a gate, cross a
road and continue on the path through the next field.
Climb over the stile and walk up steps through a wood.
Climb wall steps to emerge on the busy A259 opposite
Friston church, cross the road and take the no-through
road beside the church to Crowlink. Walk through the*

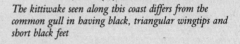

*The kittiwake seen along this coast differs from the
common gull in having black, triangular wingtips and
short black feet*

*National Trust car park, bear right and follow the road
through Crowlink to a grassy gated track, which leads
to a dewpond. There ascend diagonally right to the cliff
top and continue right over the testing summits of the
Seven Sisters to Cuckmere Haven.* The Crowlink
Valley is owned by the National Trust, and all the
land covered in the rest of this walk is safe from
development. The Seven Sisters form almost as
famous a landmark on the south coast as the white
cliffs of Dover, and present a challenge to even the
most energetic walker. Cuckmere Haven is a
totally undeveloped estuary, known for its bird life.

*Descend from Haven Brow by the South Downs
Way to a raised causeway alongside the shingle beach,
and walk along to the river. Turn right on to a gravel
path, which becomes a grassy track and eventually a
concrete road, all the time heading north towards the
head of the valley and the car park.* Allow time to
visit the excellent Country Park centre at Exceat,
either before or after the walk. Appropriately
housed in a traditional Sussex barn, the centre
contains interesting displays about the Downs.

0	200	400	600	800	1		2	3	Kilometres
0	200	400	600	800	1000	1		2	Miles

SCALE 1:25 000

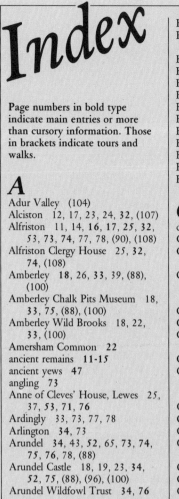

Page numbers in bold type indicate main entries or more than cursory information. Those in brackets indicate tours and walks.

A

Adur Valley (104)
Alciston 12, 17, 23, 24, 32, (107)
Alfriston 11, 14, **16**, 17, **25**, 32, 53, 73, 74, 77, 78, (90), (108)
Alfriston Clergy House **25**, **32**, 74, (108)
Amberley 18, 26, **33**, 39, (88), (100)
Amberley Chalk Pits Museum 18, 33, 75, (88), (100)
Amberley Wild Brooks 18, 22, 33, (100)
Amersham Common 22
ancient remains **11-15**
ancient yews 47
angling 73
Anne of Cleves' House, Lewes 25, 37, **53**, 71, 76
Ardingly 33, 73, 77, 78
Arlington 34, 73
Arundel 34, 43, **52**, **65**, 73, 74, 75, 76, 78, (88)
Arundel Castle 18, 19, 23, **34**, **52**, 75, (88), (96), (100)
Arundel Wildfowl Trust 34, 76

B

Barbican House Museum & Castle, Lewes 11, 14, **52**, 76
Barcombe 35
Barlavington (98)
Bateman's, near Burwash **57**, 71, 75, (92)
Beachy Head 6, 7, 12, 13, **15**, 16, 22, 35, 70, (92)
Beeding 26, 35, (104)
Bell, Clive & Vanessa 17, 35, 57
Belle Tout Lighthouse 35, 44, (92)
Belloc, Hilaire 18, 57, 64, (101), (102)
Bentley Wildfowl Reserve & Motor Museum, Halland **49**, 76
Berwick 17, 35
Bignor 13, 18, **36**, 47, (88), (98)
Bignor Hill 18, **65**, (98), (99)
Bignor Roman Villa 13, 18, **36**, 76, (88)
Birling Gap 16, 44, 52, (92)
Bishopstone 51, (90)
Bishopstone Hill 11, 14
Bloomsbury Set 17, 35, 57
Bluebell Railway **63**, 76
boating 73
Bognor Regis **36**, 78
Bonfire Celebrations, Lewes 78
Booth Museum of Natural History, Brighton 75
Borde Hill Garden, Haywards Heath **28**, 77
Bosham 36, 51, 52, 74
Bow Hill 19, 23, 43, (94)
Bramber 15, 23, 37, 75, (104)

Bramber Castle 18, **52**
Brighton 17, 18, 26, 37, **38**, 46, 71, 73, 74, 75, 78, (90), (106)
British Engineerium, Hove **38**, 76
Brown 'Capability' 29
Buchan Country Park 77
Bullock Down 12, 13, **15**
Burgess Hill 74
Burne Jones, Sir Edward 62
Burton Mill Pond 69, (88)
Burwash **57**, 75, (92)
Bury 12, **39**, 57
Butser Hill 6, 8, 12, 16, **19**, 39
Butterfly Centre, Eastbourne 76

C

calendar of events 78
Chailey Mill 64
Chalk Pits Museum, Amberley 18, **33**, 75, (100)
Chanctonbury Ring 13, 17, 18, 23, **39**, 66, (101), (102), (103), (105)
Charleston Bottom (108)
Charleston Farmhouse 17, 57
Charleston Manor (gardens) **30**, 65, 70
Charlton .40, **65**, (97)
Chichester 10, **13**, 14, 15, 18, 19, 26, 37, **40**, 43, 71, 74, 75, 76, 77, 78, (88), (96), (98), (99), (103)
Chichester Harbour 22, 41, 52, (94)
Chiddingly **41**, 78
Chithurst 51
Cissbury Ring **11**, 12, 18, 41, 39, (102), (103)
Clayton 8, 17, **41**, 51, 64, (106)
Climping 55
Coastal Defence Museum, Eastbourne 76
Coates Manor (gardens) **30**
Cobbett, William 16
Cocking 18, 19, 41, (88)
Coolham 41
Coombes (104)
Cowdray Park, Midhurst 41, **42**, 55, 56, 73, 78, (88)
crafts 73
Crowlink 48, 52, (109)
Crown Tegleaze 18
Cuckfield 42
Cuckmere Haven 70, (107), (109)
Cuckmere Valley 35, 45, 46, 48, (90), (108), (109)

D

Danny, Hurstpierpoint **52**, 75
Denmans, Fontwell **30**, 77
Devil & Dragon 43
Devil's Dyke 12, 16, 18, **42**, **43**, (105)
Devil's Jumps, Treyford Hill 12, 18, 43
Ditchling 42, (106)
Ditchling Beacon 8, 17, **43**, (90), (106)
Downland Windmills 64
Drusillas Zoo Park, Alfriston 32, 77, (90), (92)

E

Easebourne 25, (88)
Eastbourne 16, 35, 44, 52, 70, 74, 76, 78, (92)
East Dean 44, 48, (92), (109)

East Dean (W Sx) 45, 65
East Head 71, (94)
East Marden **55**, (95)
Edburton 45
Elsted 43
Exceat 16, 45, 48, 77, (92), (109)

F

Falmer 46
Felpham 57
Findon 46, (102)
Firle 46, 57, 75, (107)
Firle Beacon 8, 9, 17, 46, 53, (90), (107)
Fishbourne 13, 47, 77
Fittleworth 47
Fletchling 48
Fontwell 73, (88), (99)
Friston 16, 48, 44, (92), (109)
Fulking 18, 24, 45, 48, (105)

G

Gill, Eric 40, 42
Glynde 10, 49, **60**, **61**, 75, (90)
Glyndebourne **49**, **60**, **61**, 78
golf 73
Goodwood 24, 28, **49**, **65**, 75, 78, (88), (94), (97)
Goring-by-Sea 57
Grange Museum & Art Gallery, Rottingdean 76
Grant, Duncan 17, 35, 57
Guildhall Museum, Chichester 76

H

Hailsham 74
Halland **49**, 76
Halnaker Mill 57, 64
Hamsey 50
Hardham 57
Hartings, The 50
Hassocks 74, 75
Hastings 14, 15, 52
Hayward's Heath 9, 60, 74, 77
Heaslands (gardens) 28
Heathfield 74, (92)
Henfield 50, 74, 77
Herstmonceux 51, 74, 76, (92)
Hickstead 78
Highdown 23, 27-28, 77
Hollygate Cactus Nursery 77
Horsham 41, 76, 77
Houghton 18, (88)
House of Pipes, Bramber 75
houses & castles 74
Hove 12, 37, **38**, 74, 76, 78
Hurstpierpoint 8, **52**, 75

I

Information Centres 74
Iping Common 22
Itchenor 52

J

Jack & Jill Windmills, Clayton 8, 17, **41**, 64, (106)
Jekyll, Gertrude 27, 30
Jevington 17, 52, (109)

K

Kingley Vale National Nature Reserve 21, 43, 47, 77

King's Land 64, (101)
Kipling, Rudyard 62, 71, 75, 92, 97

L

Lancing College 18, 75, 76, (104)
Langstone Harbour (94)
Lavant Valley 26, 69
Leonardslee, nr Horsham 28-29, 71, 77
Levin Down (97)
Lewes 9, 11, 12, 14, 15, 17, 25, 37, 45, 46, 52, 53, 62, 71, 74, 76, 78, (90)
Lindfield 54
literary figures 57
Litlington 16, 54, (92), (108)
Littlehampton 15, 54, 57, 73, 74, 76, 77
Living World Museum 45, 76
Long Man of Wilmington 17, 72
Lower Dicker 74
Lower Standean (106)
Lullington 32, (92), (108)
Lullington Heath National Nature Reserve (108)
Lyminster 43

M

Mardens, The 55
Marlipins Museum 24, 76
Mayfield 55
Mechanical Music & Doll Museum, Chichester 40, 76
Michelham Priory 56, 75, (92)
Midhurst 8, 25, 56, 78, (88)
Military Aviation Museum, Tangmere 40, (88)
Monk's House 17, 57
museums & art galleries 75

N

Newhaven 57, 62, (90), (107)
Newmarket Inn 17
Newtimber 18, 45, 52, 75, (103)
North Stoke (100)
Nymans, Handcross 29-30, 77

O

Offam 12, 50, (90)
Offham Hill 53
Old Erringham 14
outdoor attractions 76
Over Viewpoint (90)

P

Pagham Harbour 22, 63, (96)
Pallant, The, Chichester 37, 40
Pallant House Gallery, Chichester 76
Parham 18, 30, 58, 75, 77, (88)
parks & gardens 77
Peacehaven 68, (90)
Penn, William 41
Petersfield 12, 47, 58
Petworth 25, 30, 58, 75, (88)
Pevensey 52, 59, 74, (92)
Philliswood 19
Piddinghoe 59, 66
Piltdown 60
Piper, John 40, 46
places to visit 74
Plumpton 60, (90)

Polegate 75
polo 73
Portsmouth Harbour (94)
Poynings 24, 42, 43, 45, (105)
Preston Manor, Brighton 38, 75
Priest House, West Hoathly 75
Pulborough 25, 61, 73, 75, 77
Pyecombe 17, 18, 61

Q

Queen Elizabeth Country Park, Butser 12, 19, 39

R

racing 73
Rapes of Sussex 52
Redoubt Fortress, Eastbourne 76
Regency Resorts 37
Ringmer 10, 49, 61
Rodmell 17, 57, 62, 66, 68
Rottingdean 9, 57, 62, 76, (90)
Royal Pavilion, Brighton 37, 38, 76

S

Saddlescombe 18
Saddlescombe Farm (105)
St Botolph's Church 18, 51
St Mary's, Bramber 75
St Mary's Hospital, Chichester 75
St Roche's (garden) 28
Saltdean (90)
Saxon churches 14, 51
Seaford 17, 32, 57, 62, 74, (90), (92)
Seal's Island 63
Sedlescombe 71
Selsey 40, 63
Seven Sisters Country Park, Exceat 6, 16, 35, 45, 48, 62, 77, (92), (107), (109)
sheep farming 8-10, 15
Sheffield Park 48, 63, 76
Sheffield Park (gardens) 29, 77
Shipley King's Mill 57, 64, 77, (101)
Shoreham-by-Sea 65, 76
showjumping 78
Sidlesham (96)
Singleton 16, 26, 65, 77, 78, (88), (97)
Slindon 57, 65, (99)
Snow Hill Creek (94)
Society of Sussex Downsmen 18, 19, (102)
Sompting 14, 51, 66
Southdown sheep 10
South Downs Way 16-19, 32, 36, 41, 44, 73, (100), (102), (104), (105), (106), (108), (109)
Southease 17, 66
South Harting 19, 50, 57, 75
South Stoke (100)
Spring Hill Wildfowl 77
Stane Street 18, 36, 52, 61, 65, (98), (99)
Stanmer Park 46, (90)
Stanstead Park 75
Steyning 14, 18, 25, 26, 57, 66, 73, (104)
Stoke (100)
stoolball 33
Storrington 18, 67, 77, (88)
Stoughton (95)
Sullington 67, 68
Summer Down (105)

Sussex Trust for Nature Conservation 50, 77
Sutton (88), (98)

T

Tangmere Military Aviation Museum 40, 57, 76, (88)
Telscombe 68, 90
tennis 78
Tilgate Park, Crawley 77
Tillington (88)
Towner Art Gallery & Local History Museum 76
Treyford Hill 12, 43
Trollope, Anthony 57
Truleigh Hill (18), (103), (104)
Trundle, The 11, (90), (97), (103)

U

Uppark, South Harting 19, 30, 50, 57, 68, 75
Upper Beeding 37, 18, (104)
Upper Dicker 50, 75, (92)
useful addresses 78

V

Vineyard Hill (103)

W

Wakehurst Place, near Ardingly 28, 29, 32, 77
walking 73
Wartling (92)
Washington 13, 18, (102)
Watersfield (88)
Weald 6, 8, 10, 13, 16, 18, 21-22, 23-26, 28, 43, 52, 71, (101), (105)
Weald & Downland Open Air Museum 6, 26, 28, 65, 69, 77, (88), (97)
Wealden Iron Industry 71
Wealdway (walk) 17
Wells, HG 57, 68
West Burton 36, 69, 71, (88)
Westdean 16, 70, (92), (109)
West Dean 70, 77, (88), (97)
West Dean College 24
West Dean (gardens) 28, 77, 88
Westfield 71
West Hoathly 70, 75
Westmeston (90)
West Wittering 71, (94)
Whitehawk (hill) 11, (103)
Wilde, Oscar 64, 72
Wildham Wood (95)
wildlife 20-22
Wilmington 17, 72
Wilmington Priory, near Polegate 75, (108)
windmills 64
Windover Hill 11,17
Wiston House 39, (102)
Woodingdean (90)
Wood's Corner (92)
Woods Mill, Henfield 10, 77
Woolbeding 51
Woolf, Virginia & Leonard 17, 57, 62
Woolstonbury Hill (106)
Worthing 13, 14, 41, 46, 72, 74, 76, 77, 78, (103)
Worthing Museum & Art Gallery 37, 41, 61, 66, 72, 76

Acknowledgements

The Automobile Association wishes to thank the following photographers,
organisations and libraries for their assistance in the compilation of this book.

J R Armstrong 23 Map; *Bridgeman Art Library* 6 South Downs; *Brighton Museum* 12 Hove Amber cup;
BBC Hulton Picture Library 60 Glyndebourne, Opera singer, 64 Windmills; *English Heritage* 59 Sorrell reconstruction Pevensey
Castle; *Derek Forss* 7 Beachy Head, 17 Long Man of Wilmington, 48 Friston church, 89 River Arun;
Francis Frith Collection 37 Eastbourne; *The Mansell Collection* 33 Milkmaid, 43 The Devil, 47 English archer, 55 Mayfield,
57 Rudyard Kipling, Anthony Trollope, 66 Mr Trelawny, 102 Hilaire Belle; *Mary Evans Picture Library* 9 Farming at Lewes,
10 Sheep, 19 Arundel Castle, 34 Arundel Castle, 49 Racing at Goodwood, 99 Beeches; *Nature Photographers* 17 Chanctonbury
Ring (F V Blackburn), 20 Purple emperor (F V Blackburn), 21 Nightingale (C B Carver), Anemone (A A Butcher),
Bee orchid (P R Sterry), Adonis blue (R O Bush), 22 Fulmar (P R Sterry), Pagham harbour (P R Sterry),
29 Magnolia Cambelli (T D Schilling), 45 Silver-washed fritillary (D L Sewell), 53 Cowslip (J L Hancock), 108 Banded snail;
Quadrant Picture Library 78 London to Brighton car run; *Edmund Nägele* Cover

The following photographs are from the Automobile Association's Picture Library:

S & O Mathews 1 Pyecombe, 3 Dovecote, 5 View from Harting, 30 Dovecote, 32 South Downs, Market Cross,
35 Beachy Head, 38 Brighton Pavilion, Street light, Brighton Rock, 39 Chanctonbury Ring, 40 Tapestry, 41 Chiddingly,
45 Cuckmere Valley, 50 South Harting, 52 Lewes Castle, 53 Hung Tiling, Keere Street, 55 Village Sign, 60 Pub sign,
61 Pyecombe Church, 63 Sheffield Park Gardens, 64 Shipley Windmill, 65 Shoreham, 66 Old Workhouse,
67 Southease church, 71 Incised crosses, 79 Birling Gap, 88 Bishop's Palace, 89 detail Petworth, 91 Palace pier, 92 Bateman's,
92/3 Herstmonceux Castle; *Martin Trelawny* 8 View from Ditchling Beacon, 8 Jill Windmill, 9 View from Firle Beacon,
11 View from Windover Hill, Microliths, 13 Chichester Museum, 14 Burial costume, necklaces, Sompting, 15 Bullock Down,
18 Saddlescombe, South Downs Way, 23 Alciston dovecote, Shoreham, 25 Anne of Cleves' Museum, Steyning,
26 Weald & Downland Museum, 27 Highdown Gardens, 28 Leonardslees Gardens, 29 Wakehurst Place, 30 Denmans Garden,
31 Long Man, 34 Arundel Castle, 36 Mosaic, Bognor Regis, Bosham, 37 Bramber, 38 The Lanes, Brighton,
40 Chichester Cathedral, 41 Jill Mill, 42 Cuckfield House, Sign, 44 Eastbourne pier, Esplanade, East Dean, 45 Edburton,
46 Firle village, Firle Place, 47 Fishbourne Roman Palace, 48 Fulking village, 49 Glynde Place, Goodwood, 51 Trug makers,
Bishopstone, 52 Newtimber Place, 54 Lindfield, Litlington, Littlehampton, 56 Michelham Priory, Cowdray Park,
57 Newhaven harbour, 58 Parham House, Petworth House, 59 Pevensey Castle, Piddinghoe church, 61 Ringmer, 62 Rodmell,
Rottingdean, Seaford, 63 Selsey Bill, Bluebell railway, 65 Shoreham harbour, 67 Sullington church,
68 Telscombe farm, Uppark, 70 West Dean, 71 Firebacks, 72 Wilmington Priory, Worthing, 74 Alfriston, 77 Ashington,
88 Mosaic, 90 Star Inn, Firle, 93 Beachy Head; *H Williams* 6 Butser Hill, 7 Weald & Downland Museum,
12 Queen Elizabeth CP, 16 Devil's Dyke, 19 Queen Elizabeth CP, 35 Wildfowl Trust, 43 South Downs Way,
69 Weald & Downland Museum

Other Ordnance Survey Maps of the South Downs

How to get there with Routemaster and Routeplanner Maps

Reach the South Downs from Southampton, Brighton, Birmingham and Cambridge using
Routemaster Sheet 9. Alternatively use the Ordnance Survey Great Britain Routeplanner Map
which covers the whole of the country on one sheet.

Exploring with Landranger and Outdoor Leisure Maps

Landranger Series
1¼ inches to one mile or 1:50 000 scale

These maps cover the whole of Britain and are good
for local motoring and walking. Each contains
tourist information such as parking, picnic places,
viewpoints and rights of way. Sheets covering the
South Downs area are:

197 Chichester and The Downs
198 Brighton and The Downs
199 Eastbourne and Hastings

Outdoor Leisure Map Series
2½ inches to one mile or 1:25 000 scale

These maps cover popular leisure and recreation
areas of the country and include details of youth
hostels, camping and caravanning sites, picnic areas,
footpaths and viewpoints.

Outdoor Leisure Map Sheet 9 covers Brighton and
The Sussex Vale

Other titles available in this series are:

Channel Islands	Ireland	North York Moors
Cornwall	Isle of Wight	Peak District
Cotswolds	Lake District	Scottish Highlands
Devon and Exmoor	New Forest	Wessex
Forest of Dean and Wye Valley	Northumbria	Yorkshire Dales